Enjoy!
Kochen auf Englisch

Sprachtraining und Rezepte

Joseph und Betty Sykes

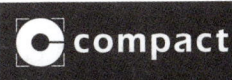

Bisher sind in dieser Reihe erschienen:

- Kochen auf Englisch
- Kochen auf Französisch
- Kochen auf Italienisch
- Kochen auf Spanisch

© 2012 Compact Verlag GmbH München

Chefredaktion: Evelyn Boos
Redaktion: Helga Aichele
Fachkorrektur: Oliver Astley
Produktion: Johannes Buchmann
Titelabbildung: StockFood, Paul Williams
Umschlaggestaltung und Layout: X-Design, München

ISBN 978-3-8174-9218-3
381749218/1

www.compactverlag.de

Vorwort

Enjoy! Kochen auf Englisch ist Rezeptsammlung und Sprachtraining in einem: 20 bekannte britische und amerikanische Gerichte zum Nachkochen sowie zahlreiche Übungen laden Sie dazu ein, mit Spaß und Genuss Ihre Sprachkenntnisse aufzufrischen.

Die vielfältige angelsächsische Küche bietet für jeden Geschmack eine große Auswahl: Von den reichhaltigen Frühstücksspezialitäten wie *English breakfast* oder *American pancakes* über schmackhafte Hauptspeisen bis hin zu exquisiten Desserts und Kuchen: Britisches und amerikanisches Essen ist einfach zuzubereiten, sieht köstlich aus und schmeckt hervorragend.

Im Anschluss an jedes Rezept können Sie anhand von abwechslungsreichen Sprachübungen Ihre Englischkenntnisse mühelos vertiefen. Unbekanntes Vokabular wird direkt auf der Rezeptseite übersetzt und kann so auf einen Blick erfasst werden. Zusätzlich bieten Ihnen Infokästen kreative Zubereitungsvarianten oder Wissenswertes zu Sprache und Landeskunde. Am Ende des Buches finden Sie ein alphabetisches Glossar, in dem Sie alle Vokabeln noch einmal nachschlagen können, sowie die Lösungen zu den Übungen.

Viel Spaß beim Kochen auf Englisch!

Enjoy!

Contents

Breakfast

Nach einem alten englischen Spruch ist das Frühstück die wichtigste Mahlzeit am Tag. Mit einer Schüssel *porridge* – Haferflocken mit heißem Wasser und Salz – waren z. B. schottische Landarbeiter auch während des rauen Winters bereit für einen Tag auf dem Feld.

Auch heute noch ist ein gutes Frühstück in Großbritannien und Nordamerika vor allem ein heißes und gehaltvolles Frühstück. Das beliebte und herzhafte *English cooked breakfast* essen die Briten zwar nicht jeden Tag, aber oft am Wochenende, in den Ferien und als perfektes Katerfrühstück!

Die Amerikaner essen morgens gerne etwas süßer, und so werden zu *pancakes* oder *French toast* oft Ahornsirup und Heidelbeeren serviert. Auch Kaffee und Obsäfte stehen in Amerika so gut wie immer auf dem Tisch.

Traditional English cooked breakfast

Es gibt viele Varianten von warmem Frühstück auf den britischen Inseln, aber Speck und Eier sind immer dabei. Deshalb wird dieses Gericht oft einfach *bacon and eggs* genannt. Das klassische englische Frühstück ist so beliebt, dass es als *all day breakfast* in vielen Cafés und Pubs den ganzen Tag über angeboten wird.

Preparation time: 15 minutes   **Cooking time:** 30 minutes   **Serves 4**

Ingredients:

- olive oil
- 8 thick pork (or Cumberland) sausages
- 8 large mushrooms
- 4 ripe tomatoes
- 6 eggs
- 8 slices of bacon
- 1 can (400g) of baked beans in tomato sauce
- 50g butter
- thickly sliced white bread
- salt and pepper
- brown sauce or tomato ketchup

1 Heat a large frying pan at a medium temperature. Once it is hot, pour a little olive oil into the pan. Add the sausages and fry for 15 to 20 minutes. Turn the sausages occasionally. Increase the temperature slightly after the first 10 minutes.

2 While the sausages are cooking, clean the mushrooms and tomatoes, chop them in half and season with a little salt and pepper.

3 Gently heat another pan and fry the tomatoes and mushrooms in a little oil at a low temperature. After 3 minutes, turn them, season with a little salt, and fry for a further 3 minutes.

4 Add the bacon to the frying pan with the sausages and fry for 2 to 4 minutes per side, or a little longer for very crispy bacon. While the meat is cooking, heat the baked beans gently on a low temperature. Stir frequently.

5 Melt the butter in a saucepan and break the eggs into the pan. Season and fry the eggs to your liking.

6 Meanwhile, toast the bread. Butter the toast and cut it in half. Serve everything on a large plate with a little brown sauce or tomato ketchup on the side. Enjoy with a mug of milky tea.

brown sauce	eine dunkle Soße mit Tomaten und Essig, die oft zu Fleisch gegessen wird	**to increase**	erhöhen
		to melt	schmelzen
		mug	Becher
to chop	klein schneiden	**poached**	pochiert
county	Grafschaft	**pork**	Schweinefleisch
crispy	knusprig	**to pour**	gießen, geben
flavour	Geschmack(srichtung), Sorte	**scrambled eggs**	Rührei
		to season	würzen
to fry	braten	**slice**	Scheibe
gently	langsam, sanft	**to stir**	umrühren
herbs *pl*	Kräuter	**wholemeal**	Vollkorn...

Exercise 1:

Collocations. Verbinden Sie die Verben mit den entsprechenden Substantiven!

1. ☐ to increase   a) the bread
2. ☐ to chop   b) the temperature
3. ☐ to heat   c) the butter
4. ☐ to melt   d) the mushrooms
5. ☐ to fry   e) the baked beans
6. ☐ to toast   f) the sausages

Exercise 2:

Prepositions. Ergänzen Sie die fehlenden Präpositionen!

for   from   in (2×)   on   to   with (2×)

Add the sausages **1.** .... the pan and fry **2.** .... 15 minutes.

Chop the tomatoes **3.** .... half and season them **4.** .... a little salt.

Fry the mushrooms **5.** .... the fat **6.** .... the sausages.

Serve **7.** .... a large plate **8.** .... brown sauce.

WHAT'S THAT?

Cumberland sausages are thick pork sausages with various herbs and spices, including black pepper. They originated in Cumberland, a historic county in northern England. They are traditionally very long (around 50 cm), but today they are usually the size of standard pork sausages, around 10 cm. For this recipe, you can also use German Thüringer or Nürnberger sausages.

Exercise 3:

Unscramble. Bringen Sie die Buchstaben in die richtige Reihenfolge!

1. I love the smell of fried c a n o b ......*bacon*............... in the morning!

2. Many people like to t r u b e t .... the bread they eat with soup.

3. g e a s u s s a .... come in many flavours and sizes.

4. t h e i w d a b e r .... is not as healthy as wholemeal or brown, but it is still a favourite on the breakfast table.

5. o a t m o t t h e c k p u .... has a high sugar content.

6. d e a k b s b a n e .... are much more popular in the UK than in Germany.

Exercise 4:

Odd one out. Welches Wort ist das „schwarze Schaf"? Unterstreichen Sie!

1. frying pan   temperature   saucepan   mug
2. turn   add   enjoy   lacking
3. gently   thickly   crispy   occasionally
4. on the side   a little   50g   a can of
5. warmer   cooler   milder   hot
6. preheated   fry   cook   turn

DID YOU KNOW?

"How would you like your eggs?" is a very common question at breakfast time. Many people like them fried, but alternatives are scrambled eggs, poached eggs or boiled eggs. British people usually fry only one side of their eggs, but in the US, people usually fry both sides, and frying just one side is known as "sunny side up".

French toast

Der *French toast* entspricht dem deutschen „Armen Ritter", ein Gericht, das sich im Mittelalter entwickelt hat. Als Arme-Leute-Essen war es ideal, um altes Brot auf schmackhafte Weise zu verwerten. Wohlhabendere Familien würden hingegen feines Weißbrot ohne Rinde verwenden. In den USA ist *French toast* sehr beliebt zum Frühstück und als leckerer Snack.

Preparation time: 15 minutes   **Cooking time:** 8 minutes   **Serves 4**

Ingredients:

- 3 eggs
- 60ml milk
- ¼ tsp vanilla extract
- ¼ tsp nutmeg
- ½ tsp ground cinnamon
- butter
- 8 slices of stale white bread
- maple syrup

1 Preheat the oven to 90°C. Whisk the eggs together in a shallow bowl. Whisk in the milk, vanilla extract, nutmeg and ¼ teaspoon cinnamon.

2 Heat a little butter in a frying pan to a medium temperature. Do not allow it to burn.

3 Thoroughly coat 2 to 4 slices with the mixture on both sides. Allow any excess mixture to drip back into the bowl.

4 Fry the first slices for approximately 2 minutes per side, or until golden brown.

5 Transfer the cooked bread onto a plate and place it in the oven to keep warm. Repeat the process with the remaining slices of bread.

6 Sprinkle the remaining cinnamon over the cooked slices and enjoy with maple syrup.

ALTERNATIVE

If cinnamon and syrup sound a little too sweet for breakfast time, you can always try savoury French toast. Cut into the side of each thick slice of bread to create a pocket, and stuff with cheese and ham. Alternatively, make a ham and cheese sandwich with two slices of French toast and grill lightly.

DID YOU KNOW?

Maple syrup is made from the sap of various species of maple tree. Native Americans were the first to obtain syrup in this way long ago and taught the process to European colonialists in the 17th century. Today, the Canadian province of Quebec produces around 75% of the world's maple syrup.

cinnamon	Zimt	savoury	herzhaft
to coat	überziehen	shallow	flach
excess	überschüssig	slice	Scheibe
to fry	braten	species	Art
ground	gemahlen	to sprinkle	streuen
maple syrup	Ahonsirup	stale	*hier:* altbacken
nutmeg	Muskat	to stuff	füllen
remaining	übrig	thoroughly	vollständig
sap	Saft (bei Bäumen)	to whisk	verquirlen

Exercise 1:

Americanisms. Verbinden Sie die amerikanischen mit den britischen Begriffen!

American

1. ☐ French toast
2. ☐ zucchini
3. ☐ eggplant
4. ☐ candy
5. ☐ fries
6. ☐ potato chips
7. ☐ cookies

British

a) biscuits
b) crisps
c) eggy bread
d) chips
e) courgette
f) sweets
g) aubergine

DID YOU KNOW?

French toast is also known as "eggy bread" in the UK. In England it isn't as popular as across the Atlantic. In Scotland, however, savoury French toast with ketchup is becoming more and more popular.

Exercise 2:

Missing word. Ergänzen Sie das fehlende Wort, um zwei sinnvolle zusammengesetzte Begriffe zu bilden.

Beispiel: number plate tectonics (→ number plate, plate tectonics)

1. coconut .... chocolate
2. French .... knife
3. duck .... white
4. frying .... cakes
5. maple .... planting
6. ice .... cheese

Exercise 3:

Unscramble the sentences. Bringen Sie die Wörter in die richtige Reihenfolge!

1. butter   in   heat   frying pan   a   the

....

2. of   slices   thoroughly   4   to   coat   bread   2

....

3. for   until   golden brown   per side   or   2 minutes   fry

....

4. of bread   slices   repeat   with   the   the   process   remaining

....

5. cinnamon   over   the   cooked   the   sprinkle   slices   remaining

....

6. known   bread   eggy   French   is   toast   as   sometimes

....

Exercise 4:

Nouns and verbs. Die folgenden Wörter können als Substantive und als Verben benutzt werden. Füllen Sie das Gitter!

coat
cut
heat
place
process
slice
transfer

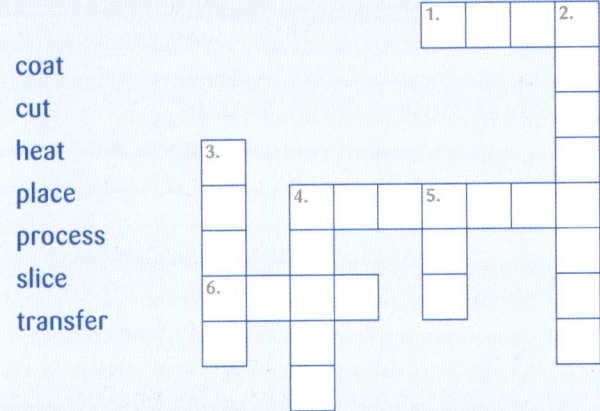

American breakfast pancakes

Pfannkuchen sind natürlich weltweit zu finden, aber die dicke Variante, die in den USA auch *flapjacks* und *hotcakes* genannt wird, ist wesentlich mit dem nordamerikanischen Frühstück verbunden. Im Gegensatz zu Großbritanninen, wo *pancakes* nur am Faschingsdienstag serviert werden, genießt man sie in den USA das ganze Jahr über.

Preparation time: 15 minutes **Cooking time:** 10 minutes **Serves 4 to 6**

Ingredients:

- 60g butter
- 2 large eggs
- 250ml milk
- 250g flour
- 4 level tsp sugar
- a pinch of salt
- 3 level tsp baking powder
- 200g blueberries
- maple syrup

1 Melt a little butter in a frying pan and pour it into a jug. Beat the eggs, then mix in the milk and a tablespoon of the melted butter.

2 Mix the flour, sugar, salt and baking powder in a mixing bowl, then gradually pour in the egg mixture and stir it well.

3 Melt a little more butter in the frying pan and heat to a moderate temperature. Pour four separate tablespoons of the batter into the pan to create four small pancakes.

4 Fry for about a minute, flip over with a spatula, then cook for another minute, or until the bottom is golden brown.

5 Stack the pancakes on a plate and cover with a clean tea towel. Alternatively, keep them warm in the oven while you cook the rest of the pancakes. Remember to add a little more butter each time.

6 Place 3 or 4 pancakes on each plate with a portion of blueberries and drizzle with maple syrup.

DID YOU KNOW?

You can also enjoy breakfast pancakes with yoghurt, fromage frais, and, if you can't get hold of maple syrup, honey.

batter	Teig	maple syrup	Ahornsirup
to drizzle	*hier:* träufeln	to melt	schmelzen
to flip over	wenden	pinch	Prise
fromage frais	Frischkäse, Quark	to pour	gießen
to fry	braten	spatula	Pfannenwender
gradually	allmählich	to stack	stapeln
jug	*hier:* Messbecher	to stir	umrühren
level	*hier:* gestrichen (voll)	tea towel *UK*	Geschirrtuch

Exercise 1:

Homonyms. Viele englische Wörter haben mehrere Bedeutungen und können unterschiedlich übersetzt werden. Kreuzen Sie die falsche Übersetzung an!

1. beat
   a) ❑ schlagen
   b) ❑ Takt
   c) ❑ Käfer

2. bowl
   a) ❑ glatzköpfig
   b) ❑ Schüssel
   c) ❑ kegeln

3. pinch
   a) ❑ klauen
   b) ❑ Feld
   c) ❑ Prise

4. honey
   a) ❑ Schatz
   b) ❑ Honig
   c) ❑ einblenden

Exercise 2:

Question and answer. Beantworten Sie die folgenden Fragen in ganzen Sätzen!

1. How much batter is needed for each pancake?

....

2. What do you use to flip the pancakes over?

....

3. What should you use to cover the cooked pancakes?

....

4. What must you remember to do each time you fry some batter?

....

5. What do you drizzle over the pancakes?

....

6. What does the recipe suggest as an alternative to maple syrup?

....

Starters

In Großbritannien sind Vorspeisen vor allem bei festlichem Essen beliebt. Wenn man auswärts isst oder die ganze Familie zu einem besonderen Anlass rund um den Tisch sitzt, hält man sich gerne an das klassische Dreigängemenü. Viele *starters* kann man auch als leckeren Snack genießen.

Wärmende Suppen sind seit jeher eine typische Vorspeise. Eintöpfe wie *cock-a-leekie* – eine Hähnchensuppe mit Lauch – und *Scotch broth* sind ebenso weit verbreitet wie Cremesuppen. In Küstenregionen werden häufig Muscheln, Lachs und Krabbensalat serviert. Darunter ist der *prawn cocktail* die klassischste britische Meeresfrüchtevorspeise. Aber auch „neue Klassiker" wie gefüllte Champignons sind heutzutage sehr beliebt.

Scotch broth

Die *Scotch broth* ist eine traditionelle schottische Suppe, die als Vorspeise oder Hauptgericht serviert werden kann. Diese deftige Brühe aus Hammelfleisch ist besonders im Winter beliebt. Man sollte für die Suppe die billigeren Hammelstücke verwenden oder kann auf Lamm- oder auch Rindfleisch zurückgreifen.

Preparation time: 20 minutes   **Cooking time:** 2 hours   **Serves 4 to 6**

Ingredients:

- 40g **split peas**
- 40g **pearl barley**
- 1 large onion
- 1 large **leek**
- 1 small **turnip**
- 3 carrots
- 2 sticks of **celery**
- 500g **neck of mutton** or lamb
- approx. 1.75l water
- salt and black pepper
- 1 tbsp **chopped parsley**
- **crusty** bread (to serve)

ALTERNATIVE

A true Scotch broth contains pearl barley. If you have difficulty finding this in the shops, why not use chickpeas for a modern twist?

1 **Soak** the split peas for 6 hours or overnight in a large bowl of water. You may also need to soak the barley – read the instructions on the packaging and soak if necessary. Alternatively, add around 30 minutes to the cooking time.

2 **Rinse** the peas and the barley. Chop the vegetables and remove any **excess** fat from the meat.

3 Place the meat in a large pot and fill it with water. **Bring to the boil** on a medium heat. Once the water is boiling, add the barley, peas, onion and a teaspoon of salt. Cover the pot with a lid and **simmer** for about an hour. **Fatty froth** will appear on the **surface** – remove this with a spoon occasionally.

4 Add the carrots, turnip and celery and **season** with black pepper. **Gently** simmer for 30 minutes.

5 Add the leek then simmer for another 30 minutes without a lid.

6 When the lamb is very **tender** and is falling off the bone, take the pot off the heat. Place the lamb on a **chopping board** and cut the meat into medium-sized pieces. Remove any skin and bones.

7 Add the parsley to the soup and season **to taste**. Serve the soup in deep bowls, and divide the meat between the bowls. Enjoy with crusty bread.

to bring to the boil	zum Kochen bringen	parsley	Petersilie
broth	Brühe, Fond	pearl barley	Perlgraupen
celery	Sellerie	to rinse	abspülen
chickpeas *pl*	Kichererbsen	to season	würzen
to chop	klein schneiden	to simmer	köcheln (lassen)
chopping board	Schneidbrett	to soak	einweichen
crusty	knusprig	split peas *pl*	Schälerbsen
excess	überschüssig	surface	Oberfläche
fatty froth	fettiger Schaum	tender	zart
flavour	*hier:* Geschmack	to taste	nach Geschmack
gently	langsam, sanft	turnip	Steckrübe
leek	Lauch	twist	*hier:* Interpretation
neck of mutton	Hammelnacken		

Excercise 1:

Crossword. Übersetzen Sie die Begriffe und lösen Sie das Kreuzworträtsel!

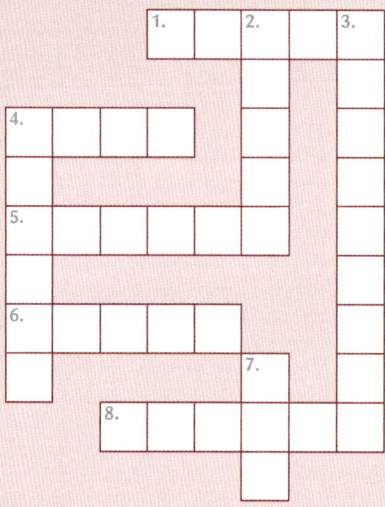

Across

1. Löffel
4. einweichen
5. Hammel
6. genießen
8. Sellerie

Down

2. Zwiebel
3. nötig
4. köcheln
7. Erbse

Excercise 2:

Noun forms. Welche Substantive passen zu den Verben? Schreiben Sie auf!

1. to require ....

2. to taste ....

3. to serve ....

4. to appear ....

5. to cover ....

6. to add ....

7. to prepare ....

8. to divide ....

> **DID YOU KNOW?**
>
> *In Scotland, Scotch broth is traditionally eaten on New Year's Day. Originally, the meat was removed from the soup and served as a second course, but today it is usually served with the broth. For extra **flavour**, cook the broth the day before you plan to eat it.*

Excercise 3:

1. vegetables	leek	celery	carrot
2. simmer	boil	add	heat
3. lid	spoon	bowl	salt
4. chop	serve	slice	cut
5. too	to	quite	very
6. and	on	beside	through

Lösung: ....

Excercise 4:

for   into   off   on (2×)   to (3×)   with (2×)

1. Bring .... the boil .... a medium heat.

2. Or add around 30 minutes .... the cooking time.

3. Cover .... a lid and simmer .... about an hour.

4. When the lamb is falling .... the bone, place the meat ....
a chopping board and cut it .... medium-sized pieces.

5. Add the parsley and season .... salt and black pepper ....
taste.

Prawn cocktail

Der *prawn* *cocktail* ist kein Getränk, sondern war in den 70er und 80er Jahren die Lieblingsvorspeise der Briten. Gegen Ende des 20. Jahrhunderts geriet der Krabben-cocktail aus der Mode, aber heutzutage erlebt er eine Renaissance als klassische britische Vorspeise.

Preparation time: 20 minutes   **Serves 4**

Ingredients:

- ½ lettuce
- 225g peeled prawns
- 4 tbsp natural yoghurt
- 3 tbsp tomato ketchup
- 2 tbsp mayonnaise
- 2 tbsp Worcestershire sauce
- 2 tbsp horseradish sauce
- 2 tbsp lemon juice
- 4 tsp chives
- black pepper
- paprika
- brown bread and butter (to serve)

1 Wash and shred the lettuce and half-fill four wine glasses or small glass bowls with it. Divide half of the prawns between the glasses. Season with black pepper.

2 In a medium-sized bowl, mix the yoghurt, ketchup, mayonnaise, Worcestershire sauce, horseradish sauce and lemon juice.

3 Spoon equal amounts of the mixture into each glass, then top with the remaining prawns.

4 Sprinkle the chives and a little paprika on top, then serve with brown bread and butter.

DID YOU KNOW?

Like with many British dishes, the secret behind the prawn cocktail is its simplicity. Many chefs have experimented with modern, exotic ingredients, but the original classic recipe remains the favourite.
"Prawn cocktail" is also one of the Brits' favourite crisp flavours along with "salt & vinegar" and "cheese & onion". But you can forget about paprika! In the UK, paprika crisps are practically unheard-of.

brown bread	Mischbrot	prawn	Krabbe, Shrimp
chive	Schnittlauch	remaining	übrig
crisps *pl UK*	Chips	to season	würzen
crunchy	knusprig	to shred	zerkleinern
flavour	Geschmack-(srichtung)	to sprinkle	streuen
		to top	*hier:* garnieren
horseradish sauce	Meerrettich (tafelfertig)	unheard-of	gänzlich unbekannt
		Worcestershire	englische Würzsauce
lettuce	Kopfsalat	sauce	aus Essig, Melasse
to peel	schälen		und Sardellen

Excercise 1:

Correct the mistakes. Finden Sie jeweils zwei Fehler in den folgenden Sätzen und schreiben Sie sie neu auf!

1. To start, shred the lettice and half-fill four Wine glasses.

....

2. Divide halve of the prawns between the glass's.

....

3. Spon equal amounts of the mixture into eatch glass.

....

4. Sprinkle the chifes on top, than serve with brown bread and butter.

....

Excercise 2:

Missing letters. Ergänzen Sie die fehlenden Buchstaben und endecken Sie einen anderen Geschmack für Chips in Großbritannien!

1. Fren __ __ toast

2. betw __ __ n

3. hor __ __ radish

4. ket __ __ up

5. d __ __ ide

6. l __ mon

> **DID YOU KNOW?**
>
> *In the UK, "chips" – as in "fish and chips" – are fried and eaten hot. These are known as "(French) fries" in the USA. If you ask for "chips" in America, you'll get a **crunchy**, salty potato snack in a packet, known as "crisps" in the UK.*

Lösung: __ __ __ __ __ and __ __ __ __ __ __

Excercise 3:

Word pyramid. Ergänzen Sie in jeder Zeile einen Buchstaben und füllen Sie so die Wortpyramide!

1. indefinite article

2. abbreviation for the US state Arkansas

3. uncooked

4. to cover, for example a gift with paper

5. edible shellfish; turns pink when cooked

Excercise 4:

Adjectives and nouns. Welches Substantiv gehört zum Adjektiv? Nur eins ist korrekt. Kreuzen Sie an!

1. equal
  a) ❏ equaline
  b) ❏ equaldom
  c) ❏ equality

2. modern
  a) ❏ modernity
  b) ❏ modernality
  c) ❏ moderndom

3. favourite
  a) ❏ favourition
  b) ❏ favouritism
  c) ❏ favoury

4. British
  a) ❏ Britishness
  b) ❏ Britishity
  c) ❏ Britishdom

5. secret
  a) ❏ secrecity
  b) ❏ secrecy
  c) ❏ secretization

6. important
  a) ❏ importation
  b) ❏ importanity
  c) ❏ importance

Stuffed mushrooms

Gefüllte Champignons wurden während der zweiten Hälfte des 20. Jahrhunderts sehr beliebt, teilweise dank der zunehmenden Beliebtheit vegetarischer Gerichte. Diese Variante mit Käse und Knoblauch findet man sehr häufig, aber andere Füllungen sind auch möglich.

Preparation time: 20 minutes   **Cooking time:** 20 to 25 minutes   **Serves 4 to 6**

Ingredients:

- 20 button mushrooms
- 2 small **shallots**
- 1 large **clove** of garlic
- 30g walnuts
- 2 tbsp **parsley**
- 15g butter
- 2 tbsp **breadcrumbs**
- 2 tbsp sherry
- 2 tbsp olive oil
- Parmesan cheese
- salt

1 Clean the mushrooms and remove the **stems** from the **caps**. Finely **chop** the mushroom stems, shallots, garlic, walnuts and parsley. Preheat the oven to 190°C.

2 Heat the butter in a frying pan over a medium heat. Add the chopped stems and shallots and **fry** for 4 minutes. Add the garlic and walnuts and **season** with salt. **Stir** well and fry for another 2 minutes.

3 Transfer to a medium-sized bowl and add the parsley, breadcrumbs and sherry. Mix well.

4 **Toss** the mushroom caps in olive oil, then **stuff** the mushrooms **tightly** with the mixture. **Grate** a little Parmesan over each mushroom.

5 Bake for 20 to 25 minutes, until the cheese is golden brown.

6 Serve immediately, either with a small salad as a starter or alone as an appetizer.

TIP

*In both Britain and America, cooks stuff mushrooms with everything from **leeks** and **blue cheese** to **spinach** and feta cheese. Why not add bacon for a meaty alternative?*

DID YOU KNOW?

*Thanks to globalization, many British and American cooks have been inspired to stuff other vegetables. In addition to mushrooms, stuffed **peppers** frequently appear on British and American menus. And stuffed aubergine (known in the US as "stuffed eggplant") is also becoming more and more popular.*

blue cheese	Blauschimmel-käse	**pepper**	*hier:* Gemüse-paprika
breadcrumbs *pl*	Semmelbrösel	**to season**	würzen
cap	*hier:* Schirm	**shallot**	Schalotte
to chop	klein schneiden	**spinach**	Spinat
clove	*hier:* Zehe	**stem**	Stiel
to fry	braten	**to stir**	umrühren
to grate	reiben	**to stuff**	füllen
leek	Lauch	**tightly**	*hier:* voll
parsley	Petersilie	**to toss**	*hier:* schwenken

Excercise 1:

Word spiral. Finden Sie die Lösungswörter und tragen Sie sie in die Wortspirale ein!

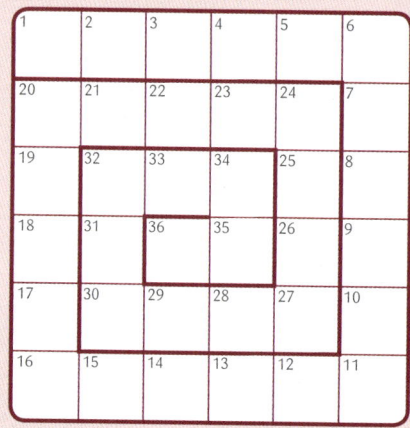

1-4: a cooking expert

4-9: In this recipe, you use a ... pan.

9-14: Beware of smelly breath!

14-17: to cut into pieces

17-24: Italian cheese used in this recipe

24-26: small, hard fruit in a shell

26-36: This recipe requires two ... of olive oil.

Excercise 2:

Unscramble and translate. Bringen Sie die Buchstaben in die richtige Reihenfolge, und verbinden Sie die Begriffe mit der entsprechenden Übersetzung!

1. ☐ v e o l c .... a) Pilz

2. ☐ l a p y r e s .... b) Parmesan

3. ☐ u b r i e g n a e .... c) Petersilie

4. ☐ s m o u h m o r .... d) Zehe

5. ☐ d r u b m s a b e r c .... e) Gemüsepaprika

6. ☐ s n a p r a m e .... f) Semmelbrösel

7. ☐ e r p p e p .... g) Aubergine

Main courses

Let's face it: Die britische Küche hatte international lange Zeit keinen guten Ruf. Und auch viele Briten selbst legten keinen großen Wert auf qualitativ gutes Essen, wichtiger war schlicht, dass man satt wurde. In den letzten Jahrzehnten hat sich aber – auch dank vielfältiger internationaler Einflüsse – die britische Küche hervorragend entwickelt.
Viele klassische britische Hauptgerichte sind perfekte Beispiele für *soul food*, also Nahrung für die Seele. Und regionale Klassiker und neubritische Gerichte beweisen, dass „britische Küche" lediglich ein Überbegriff für eine große Vielfalt von Speisen ist.

Fish and chips

Fish and chips sind überall in Großbritannien immer noch sehr beliebt und Freitag-abend ist für viele Briten traditionell *fish and chips night*. Meist kauft man diese Spezialität in einer Imbissbude, dem *chippy*. Aber es ist auch nicht schwer, das Gericht zu Hause zuzubereiten.

Preparation time: 30 minutes   **Cooking time:** 30 to 35 minutes   **Serves 4**

Ingredients:

- 225g flour
- 1 tsp baking powder
- salt
- 1 egg
- 30ml butter
- 300ml milk
- 800g floury potatoes
- approx. 1l sunflower oil for deep-frying
- 4 cod or haddock fillets
- malt vinegar
- 1 lemon

1 Sift the flour, baking powder and a pinch of salt into a large bowl. Melt the butter in a saucepan. Add the egg, butter and milk to the flour, then beat the mixture to a batter. Leave for 15 to 20 minutes.

2 Peel the potatoes and cut them into chips, which can be as thin or thick as you please. Pat the chips dry so that they do not spit when you fry them.

3 Preheat the oven to 100°C. Pour the oil into a deep pan until it is one-third full and heat to around 140 to 160°C.

4 Add some of the chips and deep-fry for 10 to 12 min-utes, until they are soft but still pale. Remove the chips with a skimming ladle and place them on a paper towel to drain and cool. Repeat with the remaining chips.

5 Dip one fish fillet into the batter and make sure it is well coated. Lower it into the hot oil. Deep-fry one or two fillets at a time for 5 to 6 minutes, then remove. Place the cooked fish in the oven to keep warm and fry the remaining fillets.

6 Once all the fish is cooked, return the chips to the oil once more and fry for 2 to 3 minutes or until golden and crispy. Shake off any excess fat and season with salt and vinegar. Serve with the fish together with a segment of lemon for squeezing.

batter	Teig	to melt	schmelzen
chips *pl UK*	Pommes	to pat dry	trocken tupfen
to coat	überziehen	pinch	Prise
cod	Kabeljau	to pour	gießen
crispy	knusprig	remaining	übrig
to deep-fry	frittieren	to season	würzen
to dip	tauchen	segment	*hier:* Schnitz
to drain	*hier:* abtropfen	to sift	sieben
excess	überschüssig	skimming ladle	Schaumlöffel
floury	mehlig	to soak	einweichen
haddock	Schellfisch	to spit	*hier:* spritzen
malt vinegar	Malzessig	to squeeze	auspressen

Exercise 1:

Collocations. Welche der folgenden Wörter gehören zusammen? Verbinden Sie!

1. baking   fillet
2. sunflower   sauce
3. cod   oil
4. skimming   powder
5. mushy   ladle
6. tartar   peas

Exercise 2:

Question and answer. Beantworten Sie die folgenden Fragen in ganzen Sätzen!

1. What must you do to the potatoes before you cut them into chips?

....

2. What do wet chips do when fried in oil?

....

3. How long do you deep-fry the fish for?

....

4. What kind of vinegar do you serve with fish and chips?

....

5. What are the three ingredients in mushy peas?

....

Exercise 3:

Plurals. Schreiben Sie die Mehrzahlform der folgenden Substantive auf!

1. chip ....

2. potato ....

3. fish ....

4. tomato ....

5. half ....

Exercise 4:

Translate. Übersetzen Sie die folgenden Sätze ins Deutsche!

1. Melt the butter in a saucepan.

....

2. Dip a fish into the batter. Make sure it is well coated.

....

3. Serve the dish with plenty of salt and malt vinegar.

....

4. Many people like to buy chips with curry sauce to take away.

....

DID YOU KNOW?

Besides lemon juice, fish and chips are often eaten with tartar sauce, curry sauce and "mushy" peas – dried peas soaked in water, then cooked to a thick green soup with salt and a little sugar.

Shepherd's pie

Dieses klassische Auflaufgericht hat sich im 18. Jahrhundert entwickelt, nachdem Kartoffeln in Großbritannien eingeführt wurden. *Shepherd's pie* war früher besonders in ärmeren Familien sehr beliebt, um aus Resten des Sonntagsbratens eine günstige und leckere Mahlzeit zu zaubern. Heute kann man die zeitlose „Hirtenpastete" auch in vielen Restaurants genießen.

Preparation time: 15 minutes   **Cooking time:** 1 hour   **Serves 4**

Ingredients:

- 1 large onion
- 1 or 2 carrots
- 700g potatoes
- 450g mince (lamb or beef)
- vegetable oil
- 2 tbsp flour
- 300ml lamb or beef stock
- 1 tbsp tomato purée
- ½ tsp mixed herbs (alternatively: thyme or parsley)
- salt and freshly ground pepper
- 25g butter
- 40ml hot milk
- 90g Cheddar cheese

1 Peel the onions, carrots and potatoes. Chop the onions and carrots finely, and cut the potatoes into chunks.

2 Fry the mince in a little oil at a medium temperature until it browns. Add the onions and carrots and fry for 5 minutes, stirring occasionally. Meanwhile, prepare 300ml stock.

3 Add the flour to the mince and continue to cook for another minute. Gradually add the stock as well as the tomato purée and herbs. Season with salt and pepper.

4 Continue stirring until the mixture thickens and begins to boil. Cover the pan with a lid and leave to simmer for 25 minutes. Preheat the oven to 190°C.

5 Meanwhile, cook the potatoes until soft. Drain and mash them with the butter, hot milk and half of the grated cheese. Season to taste.

6 Put the mince mixture in a deep ovenproof dish and cover with the mashed potato. Use a fork to spread the mash evenly and, for presentation, create a pattern of your choice. Grate the remaining Cheddar over the top and season again.

7 Bake the pie at 190°C for around 30 minutes, until the top is golden. Serve with vegetables or a salad.

ovenproof dish	Auflaufform	pastry	Teig
to chop	klein schneiden	to peel	schälen
chunk	Stück	remaining	übrig
to drain	*hier:* abschütten	savoury	herzhaft
to fry	braten	to season	würzen
to grate	reiben	to simmer	köcheln
ground	gemahlen	to spread sth.	etw. verteilen
herbs *pl*	Kräuter	to stir	umrühren
to mash	stampfen	stock	Brühe, Fond
mashed potato	Kartoffelbrei	to taste	nach Geschmack
mince	Hackfleisch	thyme	Thymian
parsley	Petersilie	twist	*hier:* Interpretation

Exercise 1:

Word search. Finden Sie 11 Zutaten aus dem Rezept!

R	P	O	T	A	T	O	E	S	C
E	E	I	K	L	S	X	Z	A	A
B	P	J	U	N	I	W	W	L	R
H	P	A	S	T	O	C	K	T	R
O	E	O	O	V	C	H	U	I	O
T	R	T	I	L	U	E	P	A	T
M	I	X	E	D	H	E	R	B	S
I	S	H	O	B	T	S	E	E	Y
L	O	N	I	O	N	E	G	O	A
K	Q	U	L	E	M	I	N	C	E

Exercise 2:

Collocations. Verbinden Sie die Verben mit den entsprechenden Substantiven!

1. ☐ grate
2. ☐ mash
3. ☐ brown
4. ☐ chop
5. ☐ stir
6. ☐ pour
7. ☐ peel

a) the wine
b) the carrots
c) the onions
d) the potatoes
e) the cheese
f) the mince
g) the mixture

DID YOU KNOW?

The word "pie" refers to many dishes, both sweet and savoury, with a pastry crust. Shepherd's pie is an exception because it is topped with mashed potato, not pastry.

Exercise 3:

Translation. Viele englische Wörter haben mehrere Bedeutungen und können unterschiedlich übersetzt werden. Kreuzen Sie die **falsche** Übersetzung an!

1. season
a) ❑ Seefahrer
b) ❑ Jahreszeit
c) ❑ würzen

2. stock
a) ❑ Brühe
b) ❑ Vorrat
c) ❑ Stock

3. ground
a) ❑ Erdboden
b) ❑ Püree
c) ❑ gemahlen

4. pepper
a) ❑ Pfeffer
b) ❑ Minze
c) ❑ Paprika

> **DID YOU KNOW?**
>
> *Shepherd's pie is traditionally made with minced lamb, but beef is frequently used today. Pies cooked with minced beef are sometimes called "cottage pies" to differentiate them from traditional lamb pies.*

Exercise 4:

Conjunctions. Ergänzen Sie die fehlenden Bindewörter!

although   and   because   but   or   until   while

1. Fry the mince .... it browns.

2. Put a cover on the pan .... leave to simmer.

3. .... the mince simmers, cook the potatoes.

4. Cook the pie until it is golden .... don't let it burn!

5. .... it isn't topped with pastry, this dish is still a pie.

6. This isn't a vegetarian dish .... it contains meat.

7. You can add stock .... red wine to the mince.

Chicken tikka masala

Dieses Currygericht hat seinen Ursprung in der Küche der vielen Inder und Pakistaner, die in den 50er und 60er Jahren nach Großbritannien einwanderten. Die Briten sind verrückt nach Curry geworden, und heutzutage sehen viele *chicken tikka masala* als *modern classic* der britischen Küche.

Preparation time: 20 minutes   **Standing time:** 1 hour or overnight
Cooking time: 25 minutes   **Serves 4**

Ingredients:

- 4 chicken breasts
- 1 red onion
- 1 clove of garlic
- a small handful of fresh coriander
- olive oil
- 1 lime
- salt and pepper
- 1 tsp chilli powder
- 1 tsp turmeric
- 1 tsp ground cumin
- 300g rice
- 250ml cream
- 2 tbsp tomato purée

DID YOU KNOW?

Traditional Indian and Pakistani dishes have been adapted according to British taste. Some people even claim chicken tikka masala was invented in Glasgow!

1 Dice the chicken breasts and finely chop the onion, garlic and half of the coriander.

2 Place the chicken in a large glass bowl with the garlic, coriander and a tablespoon of oil. Chop the lime in half and squeeze all the juice into the bowl. Season with salt and pepper. Stir well then cover with a cloth and put in the refrigerator. Leave for an hour or, if possible, overnight.

3 Heat a tablespoon of oil in a large frying pan and add the marinated chicken. Cook for around 10 minutes on a medium heat, until the chicken is well browned.

4 Remove the chicken from the pan and put to one side. Heat a tablespoon of oil in the same pan, then cook the onion and chilli powder for 5 minutes. Add the turmeric and cumin and cook for 1 minute, stirring constantly.

5 Meanwhile, boil the rice according to the instructions on the packaging.

6 Stir the cream into the spices and simmer for 5 minutes. Add the chicken and tomato purée, then simmer for a further 5 to 7 minutes.

7 Garnish with fresh coriander and serve with the boiled rice.

breast	Brust	to invent	erfinden
to chop	klein schneiden	to season	würzen
to claim	behaupten	to simmer	köcheln
clove	*hier:* Zehe	spices *pl*	Gewürze
cumin	Kreuzkümmel	to squeeze	*hier:* auspressen
to dice	würfeln	to stir	umrühren
to garnish	garnieren	taste	Geschmack
ground	gemahlen	turmeric	Kurkuma

Exercise 1:

1. teaspoon	handful	fresh	300g
2. breast	chicken	leg	rib
3. turmeric	garlic	rice	cumin
4. Birmingham	Glasgow	Newcastle	Wales
5. Pakistan	Indian	British	Italian
6. fresh	new	old	young
7. lime	onion	lemon	pear
8. false	true	real	factual

Exercise 2:

a) Squeeze the lime juice into the bowl.

b) Add another teaspoon of olive oil and fry the onion and chilli powder.

c) Remove the chicken from the pan.

d) Leave the chicken overnight.

e) Finely chop the onion.

f) Heat a tablespoon of olive oil, then add the chicken.

1	2	3	4	5	6

Exercise 3:

Missing word. Ergänzen Sie das fehlende Wort, um zwei sinnvolle zusammen-gesetzte Begriffe zu bilden.

Beispiel: frying pan pipes (→ frying pan, pan pipes)

1.	balti	....	powder
2.	chicken	....	enlargement
3.	red	....	rings
4.	hand	....	cheese
5.	cherry	....	purée
6.	olive	....	tanker

Exercise 4:

Translation. Übersetzen Sie und enträtseln Sie das Lösungswort!

1. Topf (mit Stiel) □ _ _ _ _ _ _ _ _

2. Messer _ _ _ _ _ □

3. Pfanne _ _ _ _ _ _ _ _ □ _

4. Löffel □ _ _ _ _ _

5. Kochtopf _ □ _

6. Mixer _ _ _ _ _ _ □

Lösung: □ □ □ □ □ □

Sunday roast

Nichts bringt Briten an einen Tisch zusammen wie ein guter *Sunday roast*. Seit Jahrhunderten genießen Familien am Sonntag ein Festmahl mit einem Braten und Gemüse. Die Fleischart und die Beilagen können nach Belieben wechseln, wichtiger ist der Anlass und das gemütliche Beisammensein am Esstisch.

Preparation time: 70 minutes   **Cooking time:** 2 to 4 hours   **Serves 6**

Ingredients:

- 2 to 2.5kg rib of beef
- olive oil
- salt and pepper
- 1 large onion
- 125g potatoes
- 125g carrots
- 125g parsnips
- 2 tbsp flour
- 175ml red wine
- 750ml beef stock

DID YOU KNOW?

As well as roast vegetables, mashed potatoes and Yorkshire puddings go perfectly with roast beef. To make Yorkshire puddings, make some batter (see p. 14), then pour 1cm boiling hot juice from the meat into each mould of a muffin sheet followed by 1cm batter. Cook for 25 minutes at 220°C.

1   Preheat the oven to 220°C. Rub some oil and a little salt and pepper into the beef. Peel the onion, cut it in half, and place it in a roasting tray. Put the beef on top of the onion.

2   Place the beef in the hot oven. After 20 minutes, reduce the temperature to 190°C and continue to cook for 60 minutes per kilogram for well-done beef. Baste the meat with its own juice occasionally (at least three times).

3   Peel and chop the carrots and parsnips. Put the vegetables on a roasting tray and cover them with plenty of olive oil. 30 minutes before the beef is ready, put them in the oven. They will need about an hour to cook.

4   When the meat has roasted, leave it to rest under aluminium foil. To make the gravy, first pour the meat juices into a saucepan and heat to a medium temperature. Mix in 2 tablespoons of flour and stir well. Crush the onions with a potato masher and add them to the sauce.

5   Pour in the wine and bring to the boil. Let the gravy boil for a minute and keep stirring, then add the beef stock. Bring back to boil, then simmer for 10 minutes, stirring frequently.

6   When the gravy is thick enough, pour it through a sieve into a serving jug. Discard any pieces of meat and onion.

7   Carve the beef and serve with the vegetables and gravy.

to baste	begießen	potato masher	Kartoffelstampfer
batter	Teig	to pour	gießen
to bring to the boil	zum Kochen bringen	rare	*hier:* blutig
to carve	tranchieren	rib	*hier:* Hohe Rippe
to chop	klein schneiden	roasting tray	Bräter, Bratform
to crush	zerdrücken	to rub	einreiben
to discard	wegwerfen	sieve	Sieb
gravy	Bratensoße	to simmer	köcheln
mould	Form	to stir	umrühren
muffin sheet	Muffinblech	stock	Brühe, Fond
parsnip	Pastinake	well done	gut durchgebraten
to peel	schälen		

Exercise 1:

Match up. Verbinden Sie die Begriffe mit den Erklärungen!

1. ☐ potato masher   a) to heat a liquid until it starts to bubble
2. ☐ gravy   b) to cook in hot fat or oil
3. ☐ well done   c) to cook slowly below boiling point
4. ☐ to bring to the boil   d) to cook in an oven without fat
5. ☐ parsnip   e) a long, white vegetable
6. ☐ to simmer   f) a sauce made from meat juices
7. ☐ to fry   g) fully cooked and no longer red inside
8. ☐ to bake   h) a utensil for crushing vegetables

Exercise 2:

Adjectives. Ergänzen Sie die fehlenden Adjektivformen!

1. ....thicker............. ....
2. ....most delicious...........
3. ....rare............ ....
4. ....frequent........ ....
5. ....hot............ ....

DID YOU KNOW?

Traditionally, British people like their meat well done, but more and more people in the UK now prefer the rarer continental style. For rare beef, reduce the cooking time to 30 minutes per kilogram. Medium beef requires 40 to 50 minutes per kilogram.

Exercise 3:

Vegetables. Beschriften Sie die Gemüsesorten!

1. ....

2. ....

3. ....

4. ....

5. ....

6. ....

7. ....

8. ....

Exercise 4:

Word pyramid. Ergänzen Sie die Wortpyramide!

1. A pronoun – first person singular

2. Acronym for Long Island

3. Rub olive ... into the beef.

4. to heat water to 100°C

ALTERNATIVE

Mint sauce is another British favourite to enjoy with a roast. Mix 3 tbsp freshly chopped mint with a little salt and 3 tbsp boiling water in a saucepan. Stir in 2 tsp sugar and 1 to 2 tbsp of wine vinegar when the water is still warm and mix well. Of course you can also buy the sauce ready-made.

Welsh vegetable duo

Der Lauch ist ein uraltes Symbol der Waliser. Der Legende nach trugen walisische Soldaten dieses Gemüse in einer Schlacht gegen die Sachsen an ihrem Helm, um sich zu kennzeichnen! Lauch wird in vielen walisischen Rezepten verwendet, wie in diesem Auflauf mit Karotten und Käse.

Preparation time: 35 minutes   **Cooking time:** 25 minutes   **Serves 4**

Ingredients:

- 900g leeks
- 650g carrots
- 450ml vegetable stock
- 450ml milk
- 40g flour
- 40g butter
- 75g grated Cheddar cheese
- ¼ tsp dried sage
- salt and black pepper
- 50g wholemeal breadcrumbs

1 Preheat the oven to 100°C.

2 Rinse the leeks and peel the carrots, then thickly slice both. Place the vegetables in a saucepan with the stock and bring to the boil. Cover and simmer for 15 minutes.

3 Pour the liquid into a jug. Make up to 900ml with the milk.

4 Place the vegetables in an ovenproof dish and keep them warm in the oven.

5 Melt the butter in a saucepan and add the flour. Stir in the liquid mixture and heat gently. Whisk continuously until the sauce thickens and is smooth. Reduce the temperature when it starts to boil.

6 Remove the pan from the heat, then add the cheese and sage and stir well. Season to taste with salt and pepper.

7 Pour the sauce over the vegetables, sprinkle on the breadcrumbs and grill for 5 to 10 minutes until golden brown. Serve with peas, green beans or broccoli.

DID YOU KNOW?

Toasted cashew nuts are a great addition to this dish. Take 50g cashew nuts and heat them in a frying pan over a medium heat for about 5 minutes. It is important to keep a close eye on them – if you don't, the nuts will burn!

to bring to the boil	zum Kochen bringen	to pour	gießen
dried sage	getrockneter Salbei	to rinse	abspülen
gently	*hier:* langsam	to season	würzen
grated	gerieben	to simmer	köcheln
jug	*hier:* Messbecher	to slice	in Scheiben
to keep a close	sorgfältig auf-		schneiden
eye on	passen auf	smooth	sämig, glatt
leek	Lauch	to sprinkle	streuen
liquid	Flüssigkeit	to stir in	einrühren
to make up to	*hier:* auffüllen	stock	Brühe, Fond
to melt	schmelzen	to taste	nach Geschmack
ovenproof dish	Auflaufform	to whisk	verquirlen
patron saint	Schutzheiliger	wholemeal	Vollkornsemmel-
to peel	schälen	breadcrumbs *pl*	brösel

Exercise 1:

Categories. Verbinden Sie die Lebensmittel mit der Gattung oder der Familie, zu der sie gehören.

1. ☐ leek   **a)** cheese

2. ☐ sage   **b)** dairy product

3. ☐ milk   **c)** onion

4. ☐ Cheddar   **d)** herb

5. ☐ salt   **e)** root vegetable

6. ☐ carrot   **f)** mineral

> **DID YOU KNOW?**
>
> *1st March is St David's Day, a national day of celebration in Wales. Around this time of the year, many Welsh people wear a leek to remember their patron saint, St David, a 6th-century Welsh bishop.*

Exercise 2:

Question and answer. Beantworten Sie die folgenden Fragen in ganzen Sätzen!

1. What type of cheese does the recipe recommend?

....

2. Which vegetable do you need to peel?

....

3. In which step do you remove the pan from the heat?

....

4. What goes well with this dish?

....

5. When is St David's Day?

....

6. If you decide to toast cashew nuts, what is it important to do?

....

Exercise 3:

Adjectives. Stellen Sie die Adjektive ins Gitter ein!

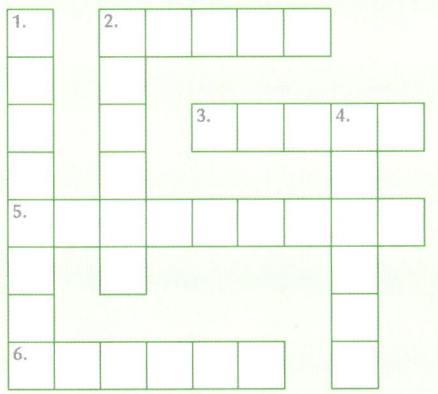

golden

great

liquid

national

ovenproof

smooth

Welsh

Exercise 4:

Unscramble the sentences. Bringen Sie die Wörter in die richtige Reihenfolge!

1. 15 minutes   and   the   for   cover   simmer   pan

....

2. oven   vegetables   the   keep   in   the   warm

....

3. the   until   sauce   whisk   continuously   is   thick   it

....

4. remove   heat   from   pan   the   the

....

5. 6th-century   was   a   Welsh   David   Bishop   St

....

6. toasted   with   cashew   go   nuts   well   dish   this

....

Bacon and cheese burger

Obwohl der Hamburger nach einer deutschen Stadt benannt wurde, ist es der weltweite Inbegriff der amerikanischen Fastfood-Kultur. Dabei ist eines sicher: die besten und leckersten Burger sind selbstgemacht!

Preparation time: 25 minutes   Cooking time: 5 to 10 minutes   Serves 4

Ingredients:

- 450g beef mince
- salt
- ½ red onion
- 1 gherkin
- 2 tomatoes
- 6 slices of bacon
- 4 hamburger buns
- 60g Emmental (or other hard cheese)
- 2 tsp barbecue sauce
- a handful of lettuce leaves

1 Roll the mince into four tight balls, then flatten them into a thick circle, around 8 to 10cm in diameter. Season each side with salt and spices as needed. Place on a sheet of baking paper and put in the freezer for 5 minutes.

2 Preheat the oven's grill function to a high temperature.

3 Cut the onion into rings and slice the gherkin and the tomatoes. Take the mince out of the freezer.

4 Cut the slices of bacon in half. Heat a frying pan to a medium temperature then cook the bacon for 6 to 8 minutes, until crisp. Turn every 2 minutes.

5 Place the burgers on a shelf and put them under the grill at the top of the oven. Grill for around 2 minutes per side for medium cooked burgers – a little less for rare, and a little more for well done. Alternatively, heat a little oil in a pan and fry the burgers for 3 to 4 minutes per side.

6 Cut the burger buns in half and grill them for 30 to 60 seconds. Keep a close eye on them so that they do not burn! Add the cheese for a few seconds to melt it a little.

7 Add lettuce leaves and gherkin slices to the bottom half of each bun, then add a burger, bacon, barbecue sauce, tomatoes, onions and finally the top slice of the bun.

bun	Brötchen	to mince	hacken
crisp	knusprig	mince	Hackfleisch
diameter	Durchmesser	rare	blutig
to flatten	*hier:* auswalken	raw	roh
freezer	Gefrierschrank	to season	würzen
gherkin	Gewürzgurke	shelf	*hier:* Rost
to keep a close	sorgfältig aufpassen	slice	Scheibe
eye on	auf	to slice	in Scheiben schneiden
lettuce	Salat	spices *pl*	Gewürze
medium	halb durch	tight	fest
to melt	schmelzen	well done	gut durch

Exercise 1:

Adjective match-up. Welche Adjektive werden gesucht? Verbinden Sie die Wort-teile und setzen Sie sie richtig ein!

re   med   ck   isp   gh   hi   ra   ght   ium   cr   ti   thi

1. Nice, ... bacon is best for this burger.

2. The burgers should be grilled at a .... temperature.

3. .... burgers require around 2 minutes under the grill.

4. Make sure the balls of mince are rolled ....

5. .... burgers are redder on the inside than medium ones.

6. The first step is to make ...., flat circles out of the mince.

Exercise 2:

Simple past. Ergänzen Sie die fehlenden Verben im Simple Past!

1. I preheat .... the grill.

2. Then, I put .... the burgers in the oven under the grill.

3. I keep .... a close eye on the burgers.

4. I cut .... the cheese into even slices.

5. I melt .... the cheese under the grill.

6. When my burger was ready, I top .... it with lettuce.

7. I also add .... gherkin slices, bacon and onions.

8. It take .... about 25 minutes for me to prepare this meal.

9. The hamburger become .... popular during the 20th century.

Exercise 3:

True or false? Markieren Sie die richtige Option und finden Sie das Lösungswort!

		true	false
1.	You must use Emmental cheese.	R	T
2.	You only need half an onion.	A	O
3.	You mustn't add salt to the mince.	C	S
4.	Both sides of the bacon need to be cooked.	T	P
5.	Minced beef steak was originally eaten raw.	Y	L

Lösung: ☐ ☐ ☐ ☐ ☐

Exercise 4:

Odd one out. Welches Wort ist das „schwarze Schaf"? Unterstreichen Sie!

1. Bordeaux	Cheddar	Emmental	Parmesan
2. ham	bacon	pork	cod
3. rocket	paprika	lettuce	watercress
4. mushroom	onion	leek	garlic
5. minute	2 o'clock	hour	week

DID YOU KNOW?

German immigrants and sailors brought the Hamburg steak to the USA in the 19th century. This beef steak was usually minced by hand, mixed with onions and breadcrumbs and served raw. It was only served as a cooked sandwich from the early 20th century, when it became more and more popular across the country with the industrialization of meat production.

Lancashire hotpot

Während der Industriellen Revolution haben Fabrikarbeiterinnen in Manchster und anderen Teilen der Grafschaft Lancashire diesen Eintopf morgens vorbereitet und ganz langsam im Ofen gegart, damit es nach dem langen Arbeitstag fertig war. Es ist heutzutage ein typisches Beispiel von *pub grub*: einfache Speisen, die in Pubs angeboten werden.

Preparation time: 25 minutes   **Cooking time:** 2 to 2 ½ hours   **Serves 4**

Ingredients:

- 900g stewing lamb
- 40g flour
- salt and pepper
- 500g carrots
- 2 medium-sized onions
- 500ml lamb stock
- 2 tsp mixed herbs
- 1 to 2 bay leaves
- green beans or peas

1 Preheat the oven to 190°C and grease a casserole dish.

2 Cut the meat into cubes and place in a mixing bowl with the flour and a pinch of salt. Mix until the meat is coated.

3 Peel the vegetables. Chop the carrots and onions into medium-sized chunks. Cut the potatoes into slices about 3mm thick.

4 Add the meat, onions, carrots and bay leaves to the casserole dish, then put the potatoes on top. Mix the herbs into the lamb stock, add pepper and then pour it over the ingredients.

5 Place a lid on the casserole and bake it in the oven. After 30 minutes, reduce the temperature to 160°C and cook for another 1½ to 2 hours, until the potatoes are soft. Remove the lid for the last 20 minutes to brown the potatoes.

6 Serve with green beans or other green vegetables.

DID YOU KNOW?

The most famous Lancashire hotpot is most certainly "Betty's hotpot" in Britain's longest-running soap opera, Coronation Street. In the programme, the character Betty worked in the Rovers Return Inn for over 40 years and was best known among TV audiences for this, her signature dish.

bay leaves *pl*	Lorbeerblätter	to peel	schälen
casserole dish	Bräter mit Deckel,	pinch	Prise
	Kasserolle	to pour	gießen
to chop	klein schneiden	signature dish	persönliche kulina-
chunk	Stück		rische Spezialität
to coat	überziehen	slice	Scheibe
cube	Würfel	soap opera	Seifenoper
to grease	fetten	stewing lamb	Lammschulter
mixed herbs *pl*	gemischte Kräuter	stock	Brühe, Fond

Exercise 1:

Sounds the same. Unterstreichen Sie die richtige Rechtschreibvariante!

1. You need almost 3 hours for / four this dish.

2. First, grease / greece a casserole dish.

3. Put the meat / meet in a large bowl.

4. Add the flower / flour .

5. Next, pour / pore in the lamb stock.

6. Serve with green beans / beens .

Exercise 2:

Translate. Übersetzen Sie die folgenden Sätze ins Englische!

1. Die Karotten, Zwiebeln und Kartoffeln schälen.

....

2. Überziehen Sie das Lamm in einer Rührschüssel mit Mehl.

....

3. Die Kasserolle in den Ofen stellen und 30 Minuten backen lassen, um die Kartoffeln zu bräunen.

....

4. Genießen Sie (es) mit grünen Bohnen.

....

5. Betty war eine Figur in einer bekannten britischen Seifenoper.

....

6. Meine persönliche Spezialität ist gebackenes Lamm mit grünen Bohnen. Es ist köstlich!

....

Exercise 3:

Ingredients crossword. Lösen Sie das Kreuzworträtsel!

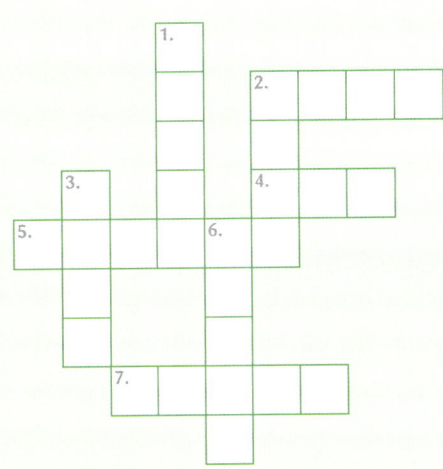

Across

2. Coronation Street is a ... opera.

4. You put this on top of a pan to keep the contents warm.

5. an orange vegetable

7. a liquid with the flavour of meat or vegetables

Down

1. a basic ingredient in bread

2. Too much of this is bad for your heart.

3. a young sheep

6. This vegetable might make you cry!

Exercise 4:

Prepositions. Ergänzen Sie die fehlenden Präpositionen!

on top of   for   into (2×)   to   until   with

1. Preheat the oven .... 190°C.

2. Cut the lamb .... cubes.

3. Put the potatoes .... the other ingredients.

4. This dish is best served .... green beans.

5. Cook without a lid .... 20 minutes or .... brown.

6. Mix the herbs .... the stock.

Cornish pasties

Die Grafschaft Cornwall im äußersten Südwestengland hat ihre eigenen ausgeprägten Traditionen und sogar ihre eigene Sprache: Kornisch. Was Kochkultur betrifft, ist Cornwall vor allem für *Cornish pasties*, herzhaft gefüllte Teigtaschen, bekannt.

> **Preparation time:** 40 minutes   **Standing time:** 30 minutes
> **Cooking time:** 35 minutes   **Serves 4**

Ingredients:

For the pastry:
- 250g flour
- 60g margarine
- 60g shortening
- 120ml water

For the filling:
- 300g beef steak
- 300g potatoes
- 150g swede
- 150g onions
- 200g butter
- salt and pepper
- thyme and rosemary
- 1 egg, beaten

DID YOU KNOW?

In the past, Cornish tin and copper miners took pasties to work with them. They were the perfect meal: the miners didn't need a knife and fork, and they could warm up cold pasties with their candles.

1   Preheat the oven to 180°C.

2   Put the flour, margarine and shortening in a food processor and blend until it has the consistency of breadcrumbs. In a mixing bowl, add the water little by little and beat with a wooden spoon until you have a soft, elastic pastry. Wrap this in cling film and leave it in the fridge for 30 minutes.

3   Meanwhile, cut the beef into small pieces. Peel the potatoes, swede and onions, then dice all the vegetables.

4   Remove the pastry from the fridge and divide into four. Roll each ball of pastry into a circle approximately 5mm thick, dusting it with flour as needed.

5   Divide the potato and swede between each pastry circle and season. Add the beef and the onion to one side of each circle, seasoning after each ingredient. Finally, put the butter on top and season one last time.

6   Brush the edges of the pastry with egg and pull the pastry over the filling to make a semi-circle. Seal the pasty tightly. Brush with the beaten egg, then bake on a tray for 35 minutes.

7   Serve with garden peas as a main course, or alone as a snack.

to blend	verrühren	pastry	Teig
breadcrumbs *pl*	Semmelbrösel	pasty	Pastete, Teigtasche
to brush	bestreichen	to seal	verschließen
cling film	Frischhaltefolie	to season	würzen
consistency	Konsistenz	shortening	Backfett
copper	Kupfer	swede	Steckrübe
to dice	würfeln	thyme	Thymian
food processor	Küchenmaschine	tightly	fest
miner	Bergarbeiter	tin	Zinn

Exercise 1:

Match-up. Verbinden Sie die Wörter zu sinnvollen Begriffen!

1. Cornish   film
2. cling   processor
3. food   bowl
4. beef   pasty
5. mixing   miner
6. copper   steak

Exercise 2:

Word search. Finden Sie 12 Zutaten aus dem Rezept!

W	A	S	N	P	E	P	P	E	R
Q	U	H	T	O	I	N	S	A	Y
C	H	O	I	T	V	L	O	B	Z
M	A	R	G	A	R	I	N	E	B
U	J	T	D	T	I	A	I	E	U
S	A	E	E	O	N	S	O	F	T
W	N	N	T	E	G	A	N	K	T
E	S	I	E	S	J	L	O	I	E
D	A	N	E	W	A	T	E	R	R
E	G	G	N	F	L	O	U	R	O

DID YOU KNOW?

In 2011, the European Commission gave the Cornish pasty "protected geographical status". This means that true Cornish pasties must be made in Cornwall.

Desserts and Cakes

Dessert, pudding, sweet, afters ... im Englischen gibt es viele Wörter für „Nachtisch". Es ist also kaum überraschend, dass dieser Gang Briten und Amerikanern sehr am Herzen liegt. Im Besonderen bietet die angelsächsische Küche viele gebackene und gedünstete Nachtische, die oft mit warmen *custard,* einer süßen Vanillecreme, serviert werden.

In der Viktorianischen Ära kam zudem der *afternoon tea* in Mode, und somit auch eine große Vielfalt an Gebäck. Heutzutage ist Backen in beiden Ländern so beliebt wie eh und je. In den USA sind *pies* geradezu kulturelle Symbole, und die Wendung *as American as apple pie* bedeutet „typisch amerikanisch"!

Bread and butter pudding

Was machen Sie mit Ihrem alten Brot? Auf keinen Fall wegwerfen! Altbackenes Brot ist perfekt für dieses ganz einfache und sehr leckere Dessert.

Preparation time: 30 minutes **Standing time: 1 hour** **Cooking time: 1 hour**
Serves 4

Ingredients:

- 300ml fresh milk
- 1 vanilla pod
- 60g butter
- 10 slices stale white bread
- 50g currants or sultanas
- 40g sugar
- ¼ tsp ground nutmeg
- 3 eggs
- 150ml fresh cream
- 2 tsp sherry
- vanilla ice cream or custard (to serve)

1 Pour the milk into a saucepan with the vanilla pod and sugar and heat gently for around 5 minutes. Do not boil. Then leave the milk to cool.

2 Meanwhile, butter the bread, chop off the crust and cut into triangles. Grease an ovenproof dish and organize the bread in rows in the dish, butter side up.

3 Sprinkle half of the currants (or sultanas) and the nutmeg over the bread, then add a second layer of bread, butter side up. Sprinkle the remaining currants on top.

4 Beat the eggs in a bowl and mix in the cream. Remove the vanilla pod from the milk and add the milk and sherry to the eggs and cream. Mix well.

5 Pour the mixture over the bread and leave to stand for 30 minutes. Preheat the oven to 170°C.

6 Bake for 1 hour until the pudding has set, then toast lightly under the grill for a crisp top. Serve hot with vanilla ice cream or custard.

DID YOU KNOW?

For many adults in the UK, bread and butter pudding brings back memories of school dinners. Even today, it is a favourite dish on school menus. Some chefs cook luxury versions with almonds and marmalade, for example, but other people say the beauty of this dessert is in its simplicity.

almond	Mandel	nutmeg	Muskat
to chop off	abschneiden	ovenproof dish	Auflaufform
crisp	knusprig	to pour	gießen
crust	Rinde	remaining	übrig
currant	Korinthe	to set	*hier:* stocken
custard	englische Vanillesoße	simplicity	Schlichtheit
to ensure	sicherstellen	to sprinkle	streuen
gently	*hier:* langsam	stale	altbacken
to grease	fetten	sultana	Sultanine
ground	gemahlen	vanilla pod	Vanilleschote

Exercise 1:

Match-up. Welche der folgenden Wörter gehören zusammen? Verbinden Sie!

1. electric
2. ice
3. vanilla
4. ground
5. ovenproof
6. stale

dish
nutmeg
oven
bread
cream
pod

Exercise 2:

Unscramble the text. Bringen Sie die Anleitungen in die richtige Reihenfolge!

a) Mix together the milk, sherry, eggs and cream.

b) Cut the bread into triangles.

c) Leave to stand before baking.

d) Heat the milk gently in a saucepan.

e) Toast for a crisp top.

f) Sprinkle half of the currants over the bread.

1	2	3	4	5	6

Exercise 3:

Simple past and past particles. Wie lauten das Simple Past und das Past Participle der folgenden Verben?

	simple past	past participle
1. to chop	....	....
2. to stand	....	....
3. to leave	....	....
4. to beat	....	....
5. to bring back	....	....
6. to ensure	....	....
7. to set	....	....

Exercise 4:

Crossword. Lösen Sie das Kreuzworträtsel!

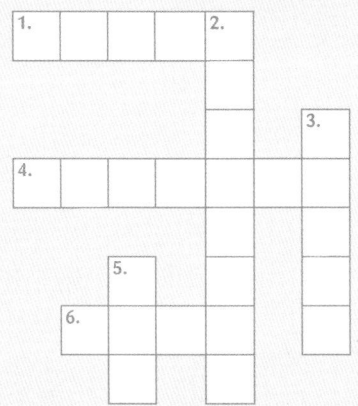

Across

1. the edge of a slice of bread
4. a small, dark dried grape
6. to heat water to 100°C

Down

2. a shape with three sides
3. hard and no longer fresh
5. the part of a vanilla plant con-
   taining the seeds

Apple and blackberry crumble

Während des Zweiten Weltkrieges stand wegen der Lebensmittelrationierung nicht genug Mehl für Torten zur Verfügung. So wurde das *fruit crumble* erfunden, wofür man weniger Mehl braucht. Heutzutage gibt es viele köstliche Varianten dieser warmen Süßspeise mit Streuseln. Weit weniger typisch ist dagegen Streuselkuchen.

Preparation time: 30 minutes   **Cooking time:** 45 minutes   **Serves 4 to 6**

Ingredients:

- 4 large cooking apples
- 200g fresh blackberries (if frozen, defrost first)
- 110g sugar
- 1 tbsp water
- 100g flour
- 75g butter
- 75g porridge oats
- 500ml custard (to serve)

1 Preheat the oven to 190°C.

2 Peel and core the apples, then chop them into large pieces. Rinse the blackberries and get rid of any stalks. Place them on a clean tea towel to dry.

3 Put the apples and 3 tbsp sugar in a saucepan with the water and cook on a low heat for 10 minutes until the apples are soft. Stir occasionally. Taste and add more sugar if necessary.

4 Mix the berries with the cooked apples and pour the mixture into a greased ovenproof dish.

5 For the crumble, sift the flour into a bowl. Cut the butter into small pieces and add it to the flour with the porridge oats. Stir in 75g sugar and rub everything together until the mixture resembles breadcrumbs.

6 Sprinkle the crumble over the fruit. Use a spoon to press down lightly on the crumble so that it is evenly spread.

7 Bake for 15 minutes, then reduce the temperature to 180°C and bake for a further 25 to 30 minutes. Meanwhile, warm the custard - or vanilla sauce if you can't get hold of custard - according to the instructions on the packaging. Serve hot.

DID YOU KNOW?

Other crumbles include rhubarb crumble, plum crumble, gooseberry crumble and raspberry crumble. Choose the fruit for the crumble according to what is in season.

breadcrumbs *pl*	Semmelbrösel	porridge oats *pl*	Haferflocken
to chop	schneiden	rhubarb	Rhabarber
to core	entkernen	to resemble	ähneln
crumble	Streusel	to rinse	abspülen
custard	englische Vanillesoße	to rub	*hier:* verkneten
to defrost	auftauen	to sift	sieben
evenly	gleichmäßig	to sprinkle	streuen
gooseberry	Stachelbeere	stalk	Stiel
greased	gefettet	to stir	umrühren
ovenproof dish	Auflaufform	tea towel	Geschirrtuch

Exercise 1:

Ingredients. Setzen Sie die fehlenden Zutaten richtig ein!

sugar   custard   flour   apples   water   blackberries

oats   butter

Core the 1. .... and get rid of any stalks from the 2. ....

Cook the apples with 3 tbsp 3. .... and the 4. ....

for 10 minutes.

Rub together the sifted 5. .... , the porridge 6. ....

and the 7. ....

Serve the crumble with hot 8. ....

> **DID YOU KNOW?**
>
> *According to a survey in 2011, apple crumble is the UK's favourite dessert. 68% of the people interviewed claimed it was the pudding they enjoyed most!*

Exercise 2:

Tastes. Ordnen Sie die Lebensmittel ihrem Geschmack zu!

cooking apples   sugar   coffee   crisps   bacon   custard

dark chocolate   rhubarb

Bitter	Salty	Sour	Sweet

Exercise 3:

Correct the mistakes. Finden Sie acht Fehler im folgenden Absatz und schreiben Sie ihn neu auf!

British people beginned to make apple crumbel while the second World War because their was a shortage of flour. Today, there is many different fruit crumbles. Why not trie using raspberries or gooseberrys?

....

....

....

....

....

Exercise 4:

Definitions. Enträtseln Sie die Definitionen und finden Sie das Lösungswort!

1. a warm breakfast dish made from oats   __ __ __ __ __ ☐ __ ☐
2. a round fruit with red, green or yellow skin   __ __ __ ☐ __
3. to pass through a sieve   __ ☐ __ __
4. to remove the hard centre of something   ☐ __ __ __
5. to mix gently using a spoon   __ __ ☐ __
6. a piece of cutlery with a round head   __ __ ☐ __ __
7. a sweet yellow sauce, popular in the UK   __ ☐ ☐ __ __ __ __

Lösung: ☐ ☐ ☐ ☐ ☐ ☐ ☐ ☐

Pumpkin pie

Der Kürbis ist heimisch in Nordamerika und ein Symbol nicht nur für Halloween, sondern auch für das Erntedankfest. Zu *Thanksgiving*, das die Amerikaner am vierten Donnerstag in November feiern, ist dieses klassische Dessert also besonders beliebt.

Preparation time: 45 minutes   **Cooking time:** 1 hour   **Serves 8**
Standing time: 2 hours 20 minutes

Ingredients:

- 500g shortcrust pastry
- 1 small pumpkin
- 175g sugar
- ½ tsp salt
- 1 tsp ground cinnamon
- ¼ tsp ground cloves
- ¼ tsp ground ginger
- 2 eggs
- 350g evaporated milk
- whipped cream or ice cream (to serve)

DID YOU KNOW?

You can use any kind of pumpkin for this pie. If pumpkins are not in season, or if you simply want to save time, you can use canned pumpkin purée in the pie. Simply ignore steps 3 and 4 and pour 300g canned purée into the mixture.

1   Preheat the oven to 200°C.

2   Roll the pastry so that it is about 3mm thick. Grease and line a 22cm pie dish with the pastry and pre-bake it in the oven for 20 minutes, then leave to cool.

3   Meanwhile, cut the pumpkin in half, remove the seeds and cut the flesh into medium-sized pieces. Put the pumpkin in a saucepan and cover with water. Bring to the boil, then simmer for 30 minutes, until tender. Drain and leave to cool before removing any peel.

4   Return the pumpkin to the saucepan and mash using a potato masher. Drain well and weigh 300g. The rest can be saved for another pie or recipe.

5   Put the sugar, salt, cinnamon, cloves and ginger in a medium bowl. Beat the eggs in a large bowl, then stir in the sugar, spices and pumpkin. Add the evaporated milk and mix well.

6   Once the pastry is cool, fill with the mixture and put the pie in the oven. Bake for 15 minutes, then reduce the temperature to 180°C and bake for a further 25 to 30 minutes. The pie is ready when a knife put into its centre comes out clean.

7   Allow to cool for 2 hours. Serve chilled or at room temperature with whipped cream or ice cream.

to bring to the boil	zum Kochen bringen	to mash	stampfen
canned	Dosen...	peel	Schale
cinnamon	Zimt	pie dish	Tarteform
clove	*hier:* Gewürznelke	potato masher	Kartoffelstampfer
to drain	abgießen	to pour	gießen
evaporated milk	Kondensmilch	pumpkin	Kürbis
flesh	*hier:* Fruchtmark	seeds *pl*	Kerne
ginger	Ingwer	shortcrust pastry	Mürbeteig
to grease	fetten	to simmer	köcheln
ground	gemahlen	to stir in	einrühren
to line	*hier:* auslegen	sweetcorn	Zuckermais
		tender	zart

Exercise 1:

Fruits. Wie heißt das Obst auf Englisch? Beschriften Sie!

1. ....
2. ....
3. ....
4. ....
5. ....
6. ....

Exercise 2:

Homonyms. Viele englische Wörter haben mehrere Bedeutungen und können unterschiedlich übersetzt werden. Kreuzen Sie die **falsche** Übersetzung an!

1. ginger
a) ❏ Gin
b) ❏ Ingwer
c) ❏ rothaarig

2. cool
a) ❏ cool
b) ❏ kühl
c) ❏ Kohl

3. tender
a) ❏ Zehnjähriger
b) ❏ Angebot
c) ❏ zart

4. serve
a) ❏ bedienen
b) ❏ Sklave
c) ❏ Aufschlag

5. well
a) ❏ Brunnen
b) ❏ gut
c) ❏ Hölle

6. thick
a) ❏ doof
b) ❏ faul
c) ❏ dick

Exercise 3:

Categories. Ordnen Sie die Begriffe richtig zu!

potato masher   ginger   knife   ice cream   pear

cinnamon   pumpkin   cream

Dairy product	Fruit	Spice	Utensil

Exercise 4:

American holidays and festivals. Verbinden Sie die amerikanischen Feiertage und Feste mit den entsprechenden Daten!

1. ☐ Thanksgiving   a) 4th July

2. ☐ Halloween   b) Fourth Thursday in November

3. ☐ Independence Day   c) Third Monday in February

4. ☐ Presidents' Day   d) First Monday in September

5. ☐ Martin Luther King Day   e) 31st October

6. ☐ Labor Day   f) Third Monday in January

DID YOU KNOW?

The central feature of a traditional Thanksgiving dinner in America is the turkey, usually eaten with mashed potatoes, sweetcorn and other autumn roast vegetables.

Sticky toffee pudding

Der *sticky toffee pudding* kam in den 1960er Jahren in Mode und ist heute ein echter Klassiker. Ein Dorf Namens Cartmel im englischen Lake District sieht sich als Geburtsort dieses köstlichen Nachtisches. Von hier aus werden *sticky toffee puddings* weltweit exportiert.

Preparation time: 30 minutes   **Cooking time:** 30 minutes   **Serves 4**

Ingredients:

- 225g dates
- 280ml water
- 1 tsp bicarbonate of soda
- ½ tsp vanilla extract
- 60g butter
- 175g sugar
- 2 eggs
- 175g flour
- 2 level tsp baking powder
- salt

For the sauce:
- 25g butter
- 225g brown sugar
- 280ml double cream

1 Preheat the oven to 150°C.

2 Remove the stones from the dates and chop them up. Put the dates, water, bicarbonate of soda and vanilla extract in a saucepan and heat to a medium temperature. Mix the ingredients together. After about 5 minutes, or when the ingredients are fully mixed, remove from the heat and leave to soak.

3 Cream 60g of the butter with the sugar. When it is light and fluffy, mix in the eggs, then the flour, baking powder and a pinch of salt, and finally the date mixture.

4 Grease an ovenproof dish and pour in the mixture. Bake for 30 minutes, or until cooked through.

5 Meanwhile, melt 25g butter in a saucepan on a low heat, then add the brown sugar and cream. Stir well and simmer for five minutes.

6 Serve the sponge pudding and pour over the hot toffee sauce. Beautiful, warm, sticky toffee heaven!

DID YOU KNOW?

Cartmel's status as "home of the sticky toffee pudding" is controversial. A restaurant in Yorkshire and a hotel in Scotland both claim that their chefs cooked and served the pudding long before the 1960s. We will never know with certainty if Cartmel is indeed the true birthplace of the pudding.

bicarbonate of soda	Natron	fluffy	*hier:* schaumig
to chop up	klein schneiden	to grease	fetten
to claim	behaupten	level	*hier:* gestrichen (voll)
controversial	umstritten	to melt	schmelzen
to cream	schaumig rühren	ovenproof dish	Auflaufform
custard	englische Vanille-soße	to pour	gießen
		to simmer	köcheln
date	*hier:* Dattel	to soak	einweichen
delicious	köstlich	sponge	*hier:* Biskuit...
double cream	Crème double	to stir	umrühren

Exercise 1:

Unscramble. Bringen Sie die Buchstaben in die richtige Reihenfolge!

1. u l f r o   ....
2. s t a d e   ....
3. f e t f o e   ....
4. n a i l v a l c a r t e x t   ....
5. w r o n b g r a u s   ....
6. g a i n b k d r e w o p   ....

Exercise 2:

Conjunctions. Ergänzen Sie die fehlenden Bindewörter!

and   but   that   until   when   while

1. First remove the stones from the dates .... chop them up.
2. .... the sugar and butter mixture is fluffy, add the eggs.
3. Bake the pudding .... it is cooked through.
4. .... the pudding is baking, make the toffee sauce.
5. Cartmel claims to be the home of sticky toffee pudding, ...
   this is not certain.
6. A hotel in Yorkshire claims .... its chef invented the pudding.

> **DID YOU KNOW?**
>
> *Sticky toffee pudding tastes delicious*
> *served with warm custard.*

Exercise 3:

True or false? Kreuzen Sie die richtige Alternative an und finden Sie das Lösungswort!

	true	false
1. This dessert contains more sugar than brown sugar.	K	S
2. Regular sugar is used to make the sauce.	N	T
3. Most of the butter is creamed with the sugar.	I	O
4. You only need a little salt for this recipe.	C	M
5. Sticky toffee pudding has a spongy texture.	K	U
6. A Scottish chef claims he invented the pudding in the 1970s.	S	Y

Lösung: ☐ ☐ ☐ ☐ ☐ ☐

Exercise 4:

Word spiral. Finden Sie die Lösungswörter und tragen Sie sie in die Wortspirale ein!

1	2	3	4	5	6	7
22	23	24	25	26	27	8
21	36	37	38	39	28	9
20	35	42	41	40	29	10
19	34	33	32	31	30	11
18	17	16	15	14	13	12

1-7: a solution derived from the vanilla pod: vanilla ...

7-15: The recipe contains 2 level ... of baking powder.

15-22: the northernmost country in the UK

22-25: a small, sticky brown fruit

25-31: The Lake District is in the North of which country?

31-39: extremely tasty

39-42: You only need a pinch of this!

Fruit scones

Scones sind ein wunderbar britisches Gebäck – und es gibt diese einfach zu zaubernde Köstlichkeit in zahllosen Formen und Varianten von süß bis herzhaft. Als Bestandteil des traditionellen *cream tea* (Tee mit *scones*, Marmelade und Sahne), einer Spezialität der Grafschaften Devon und Cornwall, ist die hier beschriebene Variante besonders bekannt.

Preparation time: 25 minutes   **Cooking time:** 10 to 15 minutes
Makes ca 15 scones

Ingredients:

- 650g flour
- 3 level tsp baking powder
- a pinch of salt
- 250g baking margarine
- 190g sugar
- 75g sultanas
- 2 eggs
- approx. 200ml milk
- butter
- strawberry jam
- clotted cream or whipped cream

> **DID YOU KNOW?**
>
> *Clotted cream is a very thick cream made by heating high-fat cow's milk, and then leaving it in shallow pans to cool slowly. Alternatively, you can use double cream or mascarpone.*

1   Preheat the oven to 220°C and lightly grease a baking tray or line it with baking paper.

2   Sift the flour, baking powder and salt into a large bowl.

3   Add the margarine and rub it into the flour until it resembles fine breadcrumbs. Stir in the sugar and the sultanas.

4   Beat the eggs in a jug. Add the milk to the eggs so that the mixture adds up to 275ml. Mix well, then gradually pour 250ml into the bowl, constantly stirring. Save around 25ml of the milk-egg mixture for glazing the scones.

5   Knead the dough a little, then place it on a lightly floured surface. Roll the mixture so that it is 1 to 2cm thick. Use a round, 5cm cutter to cut out the individual scones, then roll the remaining dough again and repeat as necessary.

6   Arrange the scones on the baking tray and use a baking brush to glaze the top of each scone. Bake for 10 to 15 minutes, until golden. Transfer to a wire rack, cover with a clean tea towel and leave to cool.

7   Serve as fresh as possible. Cut in half and serve with butter, strawberry jam and thick cream – ideally clotted cream – together with tea and milk.

baking tray	Backblech	to line	*hier:* auslegen
clotted cream	stichfester, fett- reicher Rahm	pinch	Prise
		to pour	gießen
cutter	*hier:* Ausstecher	to pronounce	aussprechen
double cream	Crème double	remaining	übrig
dough	Teig	to rub into	*hier:* unterkneten
to glaze	glasieren	to sift	sieben
gradually	allmählich	to stir	umrühren
to grease	fetten	talking point	Gesprächsthema
jug	*hier:* Messbecher	tea towel	Geschirrtuch
to knead	kneten	wire rack	Drahtgestell
level	*hier:* gestrichen (voll)		

Exercise 1:

Match-up. Welche der folgenden Wörter gehören zusammen? Verbinden Sie!

1. baking
2. tea
3. wire
4. strawberry
5. clotted
6. cream

jam
towel
cream
tray
tea
rack

Exercise 2:

Measurements. Verbinden Sie die britischen Maße mit ihren metrischen Entsprechungen!

1. ☐ 430°F (degrees Fahrenheit)
2. ☐ ½ inch
3. ☐ 1 pint
4. ☐ 1½lb (pounds)
5. ☐ 2½oz (ounces)
6. ☐ 2 inches
7. ☐ 360°F

a) 568ml
b) 180°C
c) 5cm
d) 220°C
e) 680g
f) 1.25cm
g) 70g

Exercise 3:

Prepositions. Ergänzen Sie die fehlenden Präpositionen!

for   in   into   of   on   to   with (2×)

1. Sieve the flour .... a large bowl and stir .... the sugar.
2. Add the milk .... the eggs. Save 25ml .... the milk-egg mixture.
3. Place the dough .... a floured surface.
4. Glaze the scone .... a brush and bake .... 10–15 minutes.
5. Serve together .... tea and milk.

Exercise 4:

Word pyramid. Ergänzen Sie die Wortpyramide!

1. Not to be confused with zero!
2. the opposite of "off"
3. a parent's male child
4. You smell with this.
5. an essential part of any cream tea

DID YOU KNOW?

The pronunciation of the word "scone" is often a talking point in the UK. Some people pronounce the word [skəʊn] (rhyming with "stone"), while others pronounce it [skɒn] (rhyming with "gone"). The Oxford English Dictionary recognizes both variants as correct.

Victoria sponge cake

Dieser Kuchen wurde nach Königin Victoria benannt, der am längsten regierenden Monarchin in der Geschichte Großbritanniens (1837–1901). Victoria war eine Naschkatze und lud ihre Hofdamen gerne zum formellen *afternoon tea* ein. Unter ihren Lieblingskuchen war dieser einfache Biskuit oder auch *sponge*.

Preparation time: 30 minutes   Cooking time: 35 minutes   Serves 6 to 8

Ingredients:

For the sponge:
· 200g butter (soft)
· 200g sugar
· 4 eggs
· 200g plain flour
· 4 level tsp baking powder

For the filling:
· 150ml fresh whipping cream
· ca 6 tbsp raspberry jam
· icing sugar

1 Grease a spring-clip tin and line it with baking paper. Preheat the oven to 190°C.

2 Bring the butter to room temperature, then cream it with the sugar until light and fluffy.

3 Beat in the eggs, one at a time, and add a tablespoon of flour with each egg. Then mix in the rest of the flour and the baking powder with a metal spoon.

4 Pour the mixture evenly into the tin, then transfer to the oven. Bake for about 35 minutes, until golden brown and firm. Meanwhile, whip the cream until it is thick.

5 Transfer the sponge cake to a wire rack. After 2 to 3 minutes, remove the paper and leave to cool.

6 When the cake is cold, cut the sponge in half and spread the jam over one cake, then spoon on the cream. Place the second cake on top and sift a little icing sugar on top.

DID YOU KNOW?

The Victoria sponge is associated with the Women's Institute (WI), a British voluntary organization that was established during the First World War. The Institute holds Victoria sponge baking competitions with strict rules. According to the WI, the cake may only contain raspberry jam – strawberry jam and cream mean disqualification! However, many modern recipes argue that cream is necessary for the perfect taste and texture.

baking competition	Backwettbewerb	to spread sth.	etw. verteilen
to cream	schaumig rühren	spring-clip tin	Springform
evenly	gleichmäßig	to sift	sieben
fluffy	*hier:* schaumig	sponge	*hier:* Biskuit
to grease	fetten	strict	streng
icing sugar	Puderzucker	voluntary	Wohltätigkeits-
level	*hier:* gestrichen (voll)	organization	verein
to line	*hier:* auslegen	whipping cream	Schlagsahne
to pour	gießen, geben	wire rack	Drahtgestell
rule	Regel		

Exercise 1:

Word search. Finden Sie sieben Adjektive, die im Rezept erscheinen.

F	R	O	N	Y	P	E	A	I	C	N
G	R	E	Z	C	O	L	D	O	W	F
C	H	A	U	E	A	I	F	N	L	L
A	E	T	N	T	T	G	I	L	D	U
D	O	H	N	I	J	H	Q	I	P	F
C	F	I	R	M	S	T	N	G	I	F
A	N	C	E	P	Y	E	E	U	I	Y
V	O	K	O	S	S	E	I	T	N	O
G	O	L	D	E	N	B	R	O	W	N
O	R	D	E	S	E	C	O	N	D	T

Exercise 2:

Unscramble. Bringen Sie die Anweisungen in die richtige Reihenfolge!

a) Beat in the eggs.

b) Sift icing sugar on top.

c) Put the mixture in the oven.

d) Cream the sugar with the butter.

e) While the cake is baking, whip the cream.

f) Line a spring-clip tin with baking paper.

g) Create a sandwich using the two halves of the cake.

1	2	3	4	5	6	7

Appendix

Answers

Traditional English cooked breakfast
Exercise 1: **1.** b **2.** d **3.** e **4.** c **5.** f **6.** a
Exercise 2: **1.** to **2.** for **3.** in **4.** with **5.** in **6.** from **7.** on **8.** with
Exercise 3: **1.** bacon **2.** butter **3.** Sausages **4.** White bread **5.** Tomato ketchup **6.** Baked beans
Exercise 4: **1.** temperature **2.** lacking **3.** crispy **4.** on the side **5.** hot **6.** preheated

French toast
Exercise 1: **1.** c **2.** e **3.** g **4.** f **5.** d **6.** b **7.** a
Exercise 2: **1.** milk **2.** bread **3.** egg **4.** pan **5.** tree **6.** cream
Exercise 3: **1.** Heat the butter in a frying pan. **2.** Thoroughly coat 2 to 4 slices of bread. **3.** Fry for 2 minutes per side or until golden brown. **4.** Repeat the process with the remaining slices of bread. **5.** Sprinkle the remaining cinnamon over the cooked slices. **6.** French toast is sometimes known as eggy bread.

Exercise 4:

```
              H E A T
                    R
                    A
                    N
    S   P R O C E S S
    L   L     U     F
    C O A T   T     E
    E   C           R
        E
```

American breakfast pancakes
Exercise 1: **1.** Käfer **2.** glatzköpfig **3.** Feld **4.** einblenden
Exercise 2: **1.** A tablespoon of batter is needed for each pancake. **2.** You use a spatula to flip the pancakes over. **3.** You should use a clean tea towel to cover the cooked pancakes. **4.** You must remember to add more butter each time. **5.** You drizzle maple syrup over the pancakes. **6.** The recipe suggests honey as an alternative to maple syrup.
Exercise 3: **1.** clean **2.** add **3.** gradually **4.** remember **5.** moderate **6.** other **7.** a little **8.** warm

Scotch broth
Exercise 1:

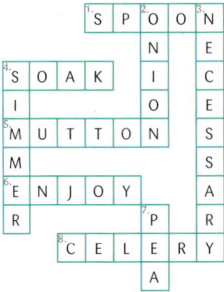

```
          S P O O N
            N     E
    S O A K I     C
    I       O     E
    M U T T O N   S
    M             S
    E N J O Y     A
    R       P     R
      C E L E R Y
              A
```

Exercise 2: **1**. requirement **2**. taste **3**. serving/servant **4**. appearance **5**. cover/covering **6**. addition
   7. preparation **8**. division
Exercise 3: **1**. vegetables **2**. add **3**. salt **4**. serve **5**. to **6**. and
   Lösung: Add salt to vegetables and serve.
Exercise 4: **1**. to, on **2**. to **3**. with, for **4**. off, on, into **5**. with, to

Prawn cocktail
Exercise 1: **1**. To start, shred the lettuce and half-fill four wine glasses. **2**. Divide half of the prawns
   between the glasses. **3**. Spoon equal amounts of the mixture into each glass. **4**. Sprinkle the
   chives on top, then serve with brown bread and butter.
Exercise 2: **1**. French toast **2**. between **3**. horseradish **4**. ketchup **5**. divide **6**. lemon
   Lösung: cheese and chive
Exercise 3:

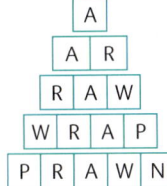

Exercise 4: **1**. c **2**. a **3**. b **4**. a **5**. b **6**. c

Stuffed mushrooms
Exercise 1:

Exercise 2: **1**. clove (d) **2**. parsley (c) **3**. aubergine (g) **4**. mushroom (a) **5**. breadcrumbs (f) **6**. Parmesan (b)
   7. pepper (e)

Fish and chips
Exercise 1: **1**. baking powder **2**. sunflower oil **3**. cod fillet **4**. skimming ladle **5**. mushy peas **6**. tartar sauce
Exercise 2: **1**. You must peel the potatoes before cutting them into chips. **2**. Wet chips spit when fried in oil.
   3. You deep-fry it for 5 to 6 minutes. **4**. You serve malt vinegar with fish and chips. **5**. The three
   ingredients in mushy peas are peas, salt and sugar.
Exercise 3: **1**. chips **2**. potatoes **3**. fish/fishes (nur bei Fischarten) **4**. tomatoes **5**. halves
Exercise 4: **1**. Die Butter in einem Stieltopf schmelzen. **2**. Tauchen Sie einen Fisch in den Teig. Achten Sie
   darauf, dass er gut/ganz überzogen ist. **3**. Servieren Sie das Gericht mit viel Salz und Malzessig.
   4. Viele Leute kaufen gern Pommes mit Currysoße zum Mitnehmen.

Shepherd's pie

Exercise 1:

R	P	O	T	A	T	O	E	S	C
E	E	I	K	L	S	X	Z	A	A
B	P	J	U	N	I	W	W	L	R
H	P	A	S	T	O	C	K	T	R
O	E	O	O	V	C	H	U	I	O
T	R	I	L	U	E	P	A	T	
M	I	X	E	D	H	E	R	B	S
I	S	H	O	B	T	S	E	E	Y
L	O	N	I	O	N	E	G	O	A
K	Q	U	L	E	M	I	N	C	E

Exercise 2: 1. e **2**. d **3**. f **4**. c **5**. g **6**. a **7**. b
Exercise 3: 1. a **2**. c **3**. b **4**. b
Exercise 4: 1. until **2**. and **3**. While **4**. but **5**. Although **6**. because **7**. or

Chicken tikka masala

Exercise 1: 1. fresh **2**. chicken **3**. rice **4**. Wales **5**. Pakistan **6**. old **7**. onion **8**. false
Exercise 2: 1. e **2**. a **3**. d **4**. f **5**. c **6**. b
Exercise 3: 1. curry **2**. breast **3**. onion **4**. cream **5**. ground **6**. tomato **7**. oil
Exercise 4: 1. saucepan **2**. knife **3**. frying pan **4**. spoon **5**. pot **6**. blender
   Lösung: season

Sunday roast

Exercise 1: 1. h **2**. f **3**. g **4**. a **5**. e **6**. c **7**. b **8**. d
Exercise 2: 1. thick, thickest **2**. delicious, more delicious **3**. rarer, rarest **4**. more frequent, most frequent
   5. hotter, hottest
Exercise 3: 1. mushroom **2**. cucumber **3**. peas **4**. potato **5**. tomato **6**. garlic **7**. aubergine (US: eggplant)
   8. (yellow) pepper
Exercise 4:

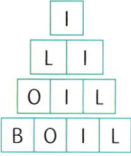

Welsh vegetable duo

Exercise 1: 1. c **2**. d **3**. b **4**. a **5**. f **6**. e
Exercise 2: 1. The recipe recommends Cheddar cheese. **2**. You need to peel the carrots. **3**. You remove the pan from the heat in step 6. **4**. Cashew nuts as well as green beans, peas or broccoli all go well with this dish. **5**. Saint David's Day is on 1st March. **6**. It is important to keep a close eye on the nuts so that they do not burn.

Exercise 3:

```
N   G R E A T
A   O
T   L   W E L S H
I   D       M
O V E N P R O O F
N   N       O
A           T
L I Q U I D H
```

Exercise 4: 1. Cover the pan and simmer for 15 minutes. **2**. Keep the vegetables warm in the oven. **3**. Whisk the sauce continuously until it is thick. **4**. Remove the pan from the heat. **5**. St David was a 6th-century Welsh Bishop. **6**. Toasted cashew nuts go well with this dish.

Bacon and cheese burger
Exercise 1: 1. crisp **2**. high **3**. Medium **4**. tight **5**. Rare **6**. thick
Exercise 2: 1. preheated **2**. put **3**. kept **4**. cut **5**. melted **6**. topped **7**. added **8**. took **9**. became
Exercise 3: 1. false **2**. true **3**. false **4**. true **5**. true
      Lösung: tasty
Exercise 4: 1. Bordeaux **2**. cod **3**. paprika **4**. mushroom **5**. 2 o'clock

Lancashire hotpot
Exercise 1: 1. for **2**. grease **3**. meat **4**. flour **5**. pour **6**. beans
Exercise 2: 1. Peel the carrots, onions and potatoes. **2**. Coat the lamb with flour in a mixing bowl. **3**. Put the casserole in the oven and (leave to) bake for 30 minutes to brown the potatoes. **4**. Enjoy with green beans. **5**. Betty was a character in a famous British soap opera. **6**. My signature dish/personal speciality is baked lamb with green beans. It's delicious!

Exercise 3:

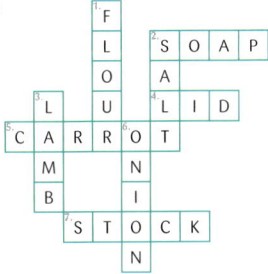

```
        F
        L   S O A P
        O   A
    L   U   L I D
  C A R R O T
    M   N
    B   I
    S T O C K
        N
```

Exercise 4: 1. to **2**. into **3**. on top of **4**. with **5**. for, until **6**. into

Cornish pasties
Exercise 1: 1. Cornish pasty **2**. cling film **3**. food processor **4**. beef steak **5**. mixing bowl **6**. copper miner

Exercise 2:

W	A	S	N	P	E	P	P	E	R
Q	U	H	T	O	I	N	S	A	Y
C	H	O	I	T	V	L	O	B	Z
M	A	R	G	A	R	I	N	E	B
U	J	T	D	T	I	A	I	E	U
S	A	E	E	O	N	S	O	F	T
W	N	N	T	E	G	A	N	K	T
E	S	I	E	S	J	L	O	I	E
D	A	N	E	W	A	T	E	R	R
E	G	G	N	F	L	O	U	R	O

Bread and butter pudding

Exercise 1: **1.** electric oven **2.** ice cream **3.** vanilla pod **4.** ground nutmeg **5.** ovenproof dish **6.** stale bread

Exercise 2: **1.** d **2.** b **3.** f **4.** a **5.** c **6.** e

Exercise 3: **1.** chopped, chopped **2.** stood, stood **3.** left, left **4.** beat, beaten **5.** brought back, brought back **6.** ensured, ensured **7.** set, set

Exercise 4:

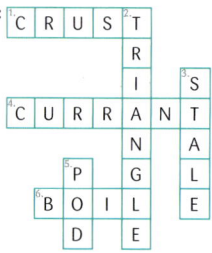

```
C R U S T
        R
        I   S
C U R R A N T
        N   A
    P   G   L
    B O I L  E
    D    E
```

Apple and blackberry crumble

Exercise 1: **1.** apples **2.** blackberries **3.** sugar **4.** water **5.** flour **6.** oats **7.** butter **8.** custard

Exercise 2:

Bitter	Salty	Sour	Sweet
coffee	bacon	cooking apples	custard
dark chocolate	crisps	rhubarb	sugar

Exercise 3: British people began to make apple crumble during the Second World War because there was a shortage of flour. Today, there are many different fruit crumbles. Why not try using raspberries or gooseberries?

Exercise 4: **1.** porridge **2.** apple **3.** sift **4.** core **5.** stir **6.** spoon **7.** custard
Lösung: delicious

Pumpkin pie

Exercise 1: **1.** orange **2.** grapes **3.** pear **4.** apple **5.** stawberry **6.** banana

Exercise 2: **1.** a **2.** c **3.** a **4.** b **5.** c **6.** b

Exercise 3:

Dairy product	Fruit	Spice	Utensil
cream	pear	cinnamon	knife
ice cream	pumpkin	ginger	potato masher

Exercise 4: **1**. b **2**. e **3**. a **4**. c **5**. f **6**. d

Sticky toffee pudding

Exercise 1: **1**. flour **2**. dates **3**. toffee **4**. vanilla extract **5**. brown sugar **6**. baking powder

Exercise 2: **1**. and **2**. When **3**. until **4**. While **5**. but **6**. that

Exercise 3: **1**. false **2**. false **3**. true **4**. true **5**. true **6**. false

Lösung: sticky

Exercise 4:

E	X	T	R	A	C	T
D	A	T	E	N	G	E
N	I	O	U	S	L	A
A	C	T	L	A	A	S
L	I	L	E	D	N	P
T	O	C	S	N	O	O

Fruit scones

Exercise 1: **1**. baking tray **2**. tea towel **3**. wire rack **4**. strawberry jam **5**. clotted cream **6**. cream tea

Exercise 2: **1**. d **2**. f **3**. a **4**. e **5**. g **6**. c **7**. b

Exercise 3: **1**. into, in **2**. to, of **3**. on **4**. with, for **5**. with

Exercise 4:

```
          O
        O N
      S O N
    N O S E
  S C O N E
```

Victoria sponge cake

Exercise 1:

F	R	O	N	Y	P	E	A	I	C	N
G	R	E	Z	C	O	L	D	O	W	F
C	H	A	U	E	A	I	F	N	L	L
A	E	T	N	T	T	G	I	L	D	U
D	O	H	N	I	J	H	Q	I	P	F
C	F	I	R	M	S	T	N	G	I	F
A	N	C	E	P	Y	E	E	U	I	Y
V	O	K	O	S	S	E	I	T	N	O
G	O	L	D	E	N	B	R	O	W	N
O	R	D	E	S	E	C	O	N	D	T

Exercise 2: **1**. f **2**. d **3**. a **4**. c **5**. e **6**. g **7**. b

Glossary

Abkürzungen

pl	Plural
sth.	something (etwas)
tbsp	tablespoon (Esslöffel)
tsp	teaspoon (Teelöffel)
UK	britisches Englisch

A

almond	Mandel

B

baking competition	Backwettbewerb
baking tray	Backblech
to baste	begießen
batter	Teig
bay leaves *pl*	Lorbeerblätter
bicarbonate of soda	Natron
to blend	verrühren
blue cheese	Blauschimmelkäse
breadcrumbs *pl*	Semmelbrösel
breast	Brust
to bring to the boil	zum Kochen bringen
broth	Brühe, Fond
brown bread	Mischbrot
brown sauce	eine dunkle Soße mit Tomaten und Essig, die oft zu Fleisch gegessen wird
to brush	bestreichen
bun	Brötchen

C

canned	Dosen...
cap	Schirm
to carve	tranchieren
casserole dish	Bräter mit Deckel, Kasserolle
celery	Sellerie
chickpeas *pl*	Kichererbsen

chips *pl*	Pommes *UK*
chive	Schnittlauch
to chop (up)	klein schneiden
to chop off	abschneiden
chopping board	Schneidbrett
chunk	Stück
cinnamon	Zimt
to claim	behaupten
cling film	Frischhaltefolie
clotted cream	stichfester, fettreicher Rahm
clove	Zehe; Gewürznelke
to coat	überziehen
cod	Kabeljau
consistency	Konsistenz
controversial	umstritten
copper	Kupfer
to core	entkernen
county	Grafschaft
to cream	schaumig rühren
crisp	knusprig
crisps *pl UK*	Chips
crumble	Streusel
crunchy	knusprig
to crush	zerdrücken
crust	Kruste, Rinde
crusty	knusprig
cube	Würfel
cumin	Kreuzkümmel
currant	Korinthe
custard	englische Vanillesoße
cutter	Ausstecher

D

date	Dattel
to deep-fry	frittieren
to defrost	auftauen
delicious	köstlich
diameter	Durchmesser
to dice	würfeln
to dip	tauchen
to discard	wegwerfen
double cream	Crème double
dough	Teig
to drain	abschütten, abtropfen
dried sage	getrockneter Salbei
to drizzle	(be)träufeln

E

to ensure	sicherstellen
evaporated milk	Kondensmilch
even(ly)	gleich(mäßig)
excess	überschüssig

F

fatty froth	fettiger Schaum
to flatten	flach drücken
flavour	Geschmack-(srichtung), Sorte
flesh	Fruchtmark
to flip over	wenden
floury	mehlig
fluffy	*hier:* schaumig
food processor	Küchenmaschine
freezer	Gefrierschrank
fromage frais	Frischkäse; Quark
to fry	braten

G

to garnish	garnieren
gently	langsam, sanft
gherkin	Gewürzgurke
ginger	Ingwer
to glaze	glasieren
gooseberry	Stachelbeere
gradually	allmählich
to grate	reiben
grated	gerieben
gravy	Bratensoße
to grease	(ein)fetten
greased	gefettet
ground	gemahlen

H

haddock	Schellfisch
herbs *pl*	Kräuter
horseradish sauce	Meerrettich (tafelfertig)

I

icing sugar	Puderzucker
to increase	erhöhen
to invent	erfinden

J

jug	Messbecher

K

to keep a close eye on	sorgfältig aufpassen auf
to knead	kneten

L

leek	Lauch
lettuce	(Kopf-)Salat
level	gestrichen (voll)
to line	auslegen
liquid	Flüssigkeit

M

to make up to	auffüllen
malt vinegar	Malzessig
maple syrup	Ahornsirup
to mash	stampfen
mashed potato	Kartoffelbrei
medium	halb durch

to melt	schmelzen	to resemble	ähneln
mince	Hackfleisch	rhubarb	Rhabarber
to mince	hacken	rib	(Hohe) Rippe
miner	Bergarbeiter	to rinse	abspülen
mixed herbs *pl*	gemischte Kräuter	roasting tray	Bräter, Bratform
mould	Form	to rub	verkneten
muffin sheet	Muffinblech	to rub into	unterkneten
mug	Becher	rule	Regel

N

neck of mutton	Hammelnacken	sap	Saft (bei Bäumen)
nutmeg	Muskat	savoury	herzhaft
		scrambled eggs *pl*	Rührei

S

O

ovenproof dish	Auflaufform	to seal	verschließen
		to season	würzen
		seeds *pl*	Kerne

P

		segment	Stück, Schnitz
parsley	Petersilie	to set (set, set)	stocken
parsnip	Pastinake	shallot	Schalotte
pastry	Teig	shallow	flach
pasty	Pastete, Teigtasche	shelf	Rost
to pat dry	trocken tupfen	shortcrust pastry	Mürbeteig
patron saint	Schutzheiliger	shortening	Backfett
pearl barley	Perlgraupen	to shred	zerkleinern
peel	Schale	sieve	Sieb
to peel	schälen	to sift	sieben
pepper	Gemüsepaprika;	signature dish	persönliche kulina-
	Pfeffer		rische Spezialität
pie dish	Tarteform	to simmer	köcheln (lassen)
pinch	Prise	simplicity	Schlichtheit
poached	pochiert	skimming ladle	Schaumlöffel
pork	Schweinefleisch	slice	Scheibe
porridge oats *pl*	Haferflocken	to slice	in Scheiben
potato masher	Kartoffelstampfer		schneiden
to pour	gießen, geben	smooth	sämig; glatt
prawn	Krabbe, Shrimp	to soak	einweichen
to pronounce	aussprechen	soap opera	Seifenoper
pumpkin	Kürbis	spatula	Pfannenwender
		species	Art

R

		spices *pl*	Gewürze
rare	blutig	spinach	Spinat
raw	roh	to spit (spit, spit)	spritzen
remaining	übrig	split peas *pl*	Schälerbsen

sponge	Biskuit	tight(ly)	fest; voll
to spread (spread, spread) sth.	etw. verteilen	tin	Zinn
		to taste	nach Geschmack
spring-clip tin	Springform	to top	garnieren
to sprinkle	streuen	to toss	schwenken
to squeeze	auspressen	turmeric	Kurkuma
to stack	stapeln	turnip	Steckrübe
stale	altbacken	twist	Interpretation
stalk	Stiel		
stem	Stiel	**U**	
stewing lamb	Lammschulter	unheard-of	gänzlich unbekannt
to stir	umrühren		
to stir in	einrühren	**V**	
stock	Brühe, Fond	vanilla pod	Vanilleschote
strict	streng	voluntary organization	Wohltätigkeits-verein
to stuff	füllen		
sultana	Sultanine		
surface	Oberfläche	**W**	
swede	Steckrübe	well done	gut durch(gebraten)
sweetcorn	Zuckermais	to whisk	verquirlen
		whipping cream	Schlagsahne
T		wholemeal	Vollkorn...
talking point	Gesprächsthema	wholemeal breadcrumbs *pl*	Vollkornpaniermehl
taste	Geschmack		
tea towel *UK*	Geschirrtuch	Worcestershire sauce	englische Würzsauce aus Essig, Melasse und Sardellen
tender	zart		
thoroughly	vollständig		
thyme	Thymian	wire rack	Drahtgestell

Bildnachweis

fotolia: Artenauta (Kochlöffel); Stephanie Frey 5 (oben), 15; Mark Stout 5 (Mitte), 11; lynea 8; Marzia Giacobbe 17 (unten), 23; JJAVA 17 (oben), 27, 63, 71; Monkey Business 29 (unten rechts), 55; colorlife 45; sarsmis 61 (Mitte), 69
istock: Nikki Bidgood 61 (unten), 79; Mark Gillow 61 (oben), 83
shutterstock: Daisy Daisy 5 (unten), 7; msheldrake 35; Monkey Business Images 39; Antonino D'Anna 47; Bratwustle 59; David Gilbey Photography 75
stockfood: Jonathan Pollock 17 (Mitte), 19; Paul Williams 29 (oben), 31; Jim Scherer 29 (unten links), 43; Food Image Source/John Kelly 29 (Mitte), 51

Mit Sprachen glänzen – SilverLine
Für Schule und Beruf

**189 Titel
21 Reihen**

SilverLine Sofort sprechen

SilverLine Lernbox

SilverLine Fit for Business English

SilverLine Kochbuch zum Sprachenlernen

SilverLine Sprachkurs

SilverLine Die 2000 wichtigsten Wörter

SilverLine Audio perfekt

SilverLine … leicht gemacht!

SilverLine Chinesisch für Einsteiger

SilverLine Schnell-Lern-Kurs

SilverLine Kurzgrammatik

SilverLine Bildwörterbuch

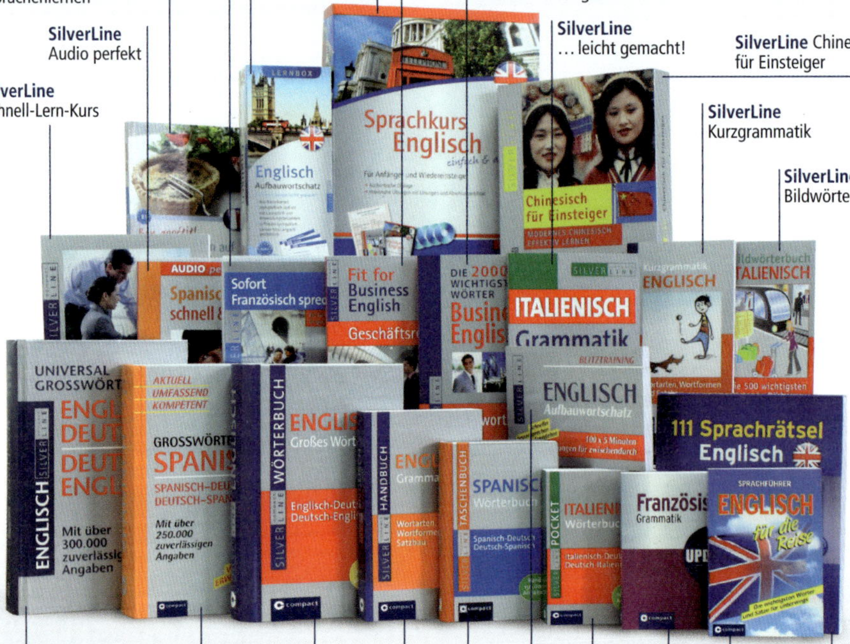

SilverLine Universal Großwörterbuch

SilverLine Großwörterbuch

SilverLine Großes Wörterbuch

SilverLine PVC

SilverLine Taschenbuch

SilverLine Pocket

SilverLine Blitztraining

SilverLine Update

SilverLine Sprachführer für die Reise

SilverLine 111 Sprachrätsel

Compact Verlag GmbH
Baierbrunner Str. 27 · 81379 München · Tel. 0 89/74 51 61-0 · Fax 0 89/75 60 95
www.compactverlag.de · www.lernkrimi.de